THE CONSULTANT'S GUIDE TO PUBLICITY

D1396945

THE CONSULTANT'S GUIDE TO PUBLICITY

How to Make a Name for Yourself by Promoting Your Expertise

REECE FRANKLIN

JOHN WILEY & SONS, INC.

New York · Chichester · Brisbane · Toronto · Singapore

Publisher: James Childs
Editor: Ruth Mills
Managing Editor: Linda Indig
Composition: Impressions Book and Journal Services, Inc.

This text is printed on acid-free paper.

Library of Congress Cataloging-in-Publication Data:

Franklin, Reece A.
    The consultant's guide to publicity : how to make a name for
yourself by promoting your expertise / Reece Franklin.
        p.   cm.
    Includes bibliographical references.
    ISBN 0-471-12619-5 (cloth / alk. paper). — ISBN 0-471-12621-7 (pbk. :
alk. paper)
    1. Consultants—Marketing.   2. Public relations.   3. Publicity.
I. Title.
HD69.C6F73   1996
001'.068'8—dc20   95-45913

Printed in the United States of America

10 9 8 7 6 5 4 3 2 1

CONTENTS

CONTENTS

Appendixes

Introduction

Today's consultant is a master of the most complex disciplines ever developed. He or she must be a marketer, a confidant to clients, a service technician, a computer wizard, and a magician all rolled into one.

And normally it's the marketing that gets short shrift in any consultant's practice. "I've no time for marketing full-time," many consultants tell me. "One hour a day is max, all that I can afford. So what technique should I use?"

My answer? Try doing some publicity two or three times a week. Yet when I mention this tactic, many consultants look at me like I'm some creature from a Martian colony.

"Publicity? Consultants don't do publicity. That's for products and major corporations with big budgets!" Oh, really?

INTRODUCTION

Let me tell you something. Consultants do publicity, and in a big, big way. Want to know why? IT GETS THEM CLIENTS AND NEW BUSINESS. PERIOD.

FRONT-PAGE HERO

Let me tell you a story about a colleague of mine (I'll call him Mitch—not his real name). Mitch is an investment advisor (read "consultant") in Orange County, California. He's had his share of small stories and a few big hits. Not long ago he enrolled in a seminar I gave on free publicity (the precursor to this book). Afterward he tried one of the simple techniques I suggested—"Going down to meet them"—which you'll learn about later on in this book.

Two weeks later, Mitch sent me a clipping from the front page of the *Orange County Register* business section with himself as the featured player and a four-color picture.

That was a year ago. Since then, Mitch has become the featured guru for the *Register* on anything financial. And his clients? Current ones were impressed, and new prospects say they want "the guy the *Register* quotes"!

So don't tell me publicity is not for you—IT IS! You'll be able to use it to build your business. You'll use it to hone your finely crafted expert image. You'll gain credibility, respect, and reputation as someone who's more than "just a consultant." You'll become THE leading local or regional consultant and expert on your industry.

WHO I'M WRITING FOR

If you're like the consultants mentioned above, this book is about to change the way you think about publicity as a marketing tool forever!

It's for those of you who've never done any publicity, the "great unwashed" out there. It's for those of you who've tried a press release or two and maybe received one or two stories out of 50 or 100 press releases sent—a horrible batting average. It's even for those consultants who've tried consistently yet still keep missing their goals.

Finally, it's for those of you who've wanted to understand the process completely and need a road map to guide you.

YOU NEED TO PLAN

With any project the good consultant sets up a plan of attack, using all the research methods and analysis tools at his or her disposal. So it is with publicity as well.

Think of your publicity campaign as another project for a client. In fact, the most important client you have—you. As with any project, we'll design a plan that takes into account the personality, the strengths, the weaknesses, and the special characteristics of the client—their history and the goals and objectives they want to accomplish.

Then we'll do our core research, finding out facts and information we can use to build our case.

Next we'll look at our client's customers (in this case, the editors and reporters who decide whether to use or write our client's story) to find out what their needs and wants are.

We'll continue by setting a budget and calendar to specifically determine how much to spend and when to spend it.

Lastly we'll write our report (the press material) and track the implementation (how many stories were printed or broadcast).

WHO IS REECE FRANKLIN, AND WHY IS HE WRITING THIS BOOK?

Let me answer that by telling you who I'm not.

I'm not an academic with an M.B.A. or a Ph.D. Sorry, I have just a bachelor's degree from 25 years ago. (It seems to have done quite well for me all these years, though.)

I'm not a high-priced Madison Avenue publicist with hundreds of Fortune 500 or 1000 clients, trying to impress you with my wealth of knowledge. Nor do I believe that high-level publicity, the kind done by the Procter and Gambles of the world, necessarily translates to your type of business, or to your clients'.

I'm not a Hollywood agent or publicist with major actors for clients. Please—I don't even like to drive to Hollywood on my days off.

I'm just your average small-business consultant who happens to specialize in publicity and advertising. I run a one-person shop, perhaps like many of you do. In fact, I work out of my home.

And the clients I work with? Other consultants, small businesses, entrepreneurs, and so on. Along the way I've managed to get quite a bit of publicity for them—and, I'm happy to say, for myself.

The techniques? No tricks, no stunts, no gimmicks. (Well, maybe one or two "events" that helped position me—you'll read about it later on.)

Just the basic what works, what doesn't, and why.

You see, there's a distinct difference between publicity for products and retailers and publicity for services and consultants. In fact, consultant publicity is a whole different ball game.

Most of you want to maintain a professional image and won't go in for any schemes, stunts, or retail techniques that may make you look like a huckster. And I don't blame you.

Yet you want results!

The techniques in this book will show you how to get results, I guarantee that (assuming you follow the guidelines exactly).

Can I prove these techniques work? You bet.

Sprinkled liberally throughout this book are many examples of publicity campaigns and methods that have worked. They're not made up, but really happened to students or clients of mine.

WHAT'S INSIDE?

Chapter 1 explores the pros and cons of doing publicity yourself, or turning to high-cost public relations firms. Chapter 2 lays the groundwork for your activities as a self-publicist, setting objectives and goals and defining the terms you'll need to know.

Chapter 3, the meat and potatoes, gets into the actual planning process. Chapter 4 shows you how to develop unique story ideas or angles, the quintessential element necessary for success.

Chapter 5 covers basic housekeeping, like setting up media contact files and the press kit. In Chapter 6, we'll discuss in depth 28 different tools for working the publicity game.

Chapter 7, *"Dealing with the Media,"* is numero uno on your hit parade. If you study nothing else in this book, get to know this chapter. In fact, I suggest you read it FIRST, then go back and start the book from Chapter 1.

Those of you with *Oprah* fever in your veins will want to explore Chapter 8, on television and radio interviews. What to do if you slip up and need emergency or panic publicity is covered in Chapter 9.

Finally, the all-important tracking of results, which *can* and *must* be done in publicity, is covered in Chapter 10.

HOW TO USE THIS BOOK

Read each chapter first by skimming the heads and subheads to get a feel for what's in store. Use a highlighter to emphasize anything you want to go over in depth. Then start again at the beginning of the chapter, reading each section fully until you understand the principles. Use a pen and take notes.

The worksheets, once understood, are for you to fill in for your own publicity plan.

As with any task, what you put into it is what you'll get out of it.

So now, if you're quite ready, let's get started.

CHAPTER 1

Do-It-Yourself vs. Outside Help

There are two ways you can play the publicity game—do-it-yourself or hire outside help.

Doing it yourself requires time, which you probably have in abundance; some money, which you may or may not have; and knowledge, which you will gain from this book. Hiring outside services, on the other hand, requires, again, time, more money, which you probably don't have, and the scary prospect of banking on outside knowledge.

Scary—because you never know exactly how much an outsider knows about your particular business and client base. Oh, they can learn over several months—or even years—but they're learning on your time and your money.

One of my students put it quite well: "I don't know about you, but I'd rather not spend my hard-earned dollars to teach some PR firm about my industry. Let someone else fund their learning

1

curve. I want someone who already is seasoned in my field." To this I say, "Amen."

HOW TO HIRE OUTSIDE HELP

Now, I assume you intend to do it yourself, else why read this book? But for those of you who upon finishing this tome grasp the nearest bottle of gin, take a swig, and say, "Whew, that's too much hard work—I'll hire somebody," let me give you the parameters for hiring those certain someones.

Parameter 1: Finding the Right Publicist

First, you need to find a publicist or freelancer who specializes in your industry. If your industry is small, this may be difficult since few people can afford to make a living on a small market. If your industry is large, who's the best publicist? And where do you look?

You *could* try the Yellow Pages, I suppose. But I don't recommend it. Most people don't use the Yellow Pages to find consultants, and publicists are a specialized form of consulting. In fact, I've never heard of a company hiring a publicity firm through the Yellow Pages.

Or you could try asking other consultants in your field whom they would recommend. Two problems here. First, what if they really like their publicist? You're a competitor. Do you really think they'll let you use their heavy hitter? I doubt it. You might wind up with a recommendation that's off the mark, one specifically intended to throw you a curve.

Second problem: what if they used the publicist a long time ago? How do you know this person is still good and has kept up with the changes in your field? They might not have.

So where to find someone? The Public Relations Society of America (PRSA) local chapter. They should have a list of members available for assignments; the list should also show members' specialties. One word of caution here—PRSA members do not become members based on ability. Anyone with a slight knowledge of publicity can join. My suggestion is to talk to their past clients thoroughly and get a feel for the following *imperative* criteria:

1. How long did the person work on the project? A one-shot, just-do-a-release-and-send-it-out assignment is vastly different from a long-term publicity campaign.
2. How well did they communicate with the client—did they understand the client's needs? Did they explain clearly what they would do for the client?
3. How long did the project take? Was it done on time, or did it run over?
4. How did they charge? By the hour? Project? Monthly retainer?
5. How long did it take to get tangible results? One month or one year? I've known situations where a publicist took over one year, on retainer, and got only two stories for the client in minor newspapers. Not a good track record.
6. What priority did the publicist give to the client? Did they get all excited about the project at first, then go looking for other work, leaving the client on the back burner?

A side note: In case this sounds familiar, it should. Publicists are consultants, just like us. And the criteria you use to benchmark and determine who to use is the same our clients use to determine how well we're doing. So take heed. You might decide to test your own business against the above six criteria and fix any problems.

Parameter 2: Define the Job to Control Costs

The second parameter for hiring outsiders: know what you're paying for. Make sure all the costs are spelled out *up front*. Hidden costs can kill you.

Most publicists have a fee schedule that outlines how much they charge for certain work—press releases, press kits, fact sheets, follow-up, and so on. The hidden costs, like postage, printing, press-kit covers, typography, and graphics are the ones that add up.

So when the freelancer you've decided to hire says, "Plus expenses," have those expenses spelled out in writing, with a cap. "No expenses above $200 per month may be charged to me without my *prior* written approval."

Parameter 3: Measuring Results

The third and final parameter—have a way to measure whether the outside help is successful (see Chapter 10, "Measuring Results"). Most publicity people will tell you it's an intangible and difficult to measure. Yes and no. While you can't tell how many responses or sales will come from a particular story or item about you, you *can* expect, based on how you target your media and how well the story is written, a certain amount to "hit," or get placement in the paper (or radio or television coverage).

What specifically should you expect? There's no rule of thumb because there are so many variables to your particular story—how well it is written, who you target, how you make the story angle unique, and so on. I'll just say this—it should be easy to get several stories about your consultancy in the local paper within three to four months. If not, you may have the wrong outside help.

FREELANCER VS. PUBLICITY FIRM

Freelance publicists, myself included, run the gamut from one-person operations to small boutiques with several employees. Most are former journalists or have left full-service firms to start their own shops. Many specialize in specific industries or services. One way to find a good freelancer is to call your local paper and ask who they know. In other words, who does work that they accept on a regular basis. (This is who you want: someone with a track record for getting stories in.)

4

I also suggest you try for former reporters. These people have been on both sides of the fence, the pitching end and the receiving end. (*Pitching* is selling a story to an editor or reporter.) Since they've been pitched thousands of times, they know what reporters and editors like—and don't like. With an exreporter, you're getting an insider on your team.

Most freelancers charge by the project, anywhere from a few hundred dollars for a release up to several thousand for a full-bore campaign. No matter what the fee, you can be sure a freelancer will charge you less than a full-service firm that has overhead to contend with. (For a suggested fee schedule, see Table 1-1).

Full-service public relations agencies are, for the most part, way out of your league. Unless you're a large consulting firm yourself, stay away from the top guns. You don't have the money they require for a retainer, so they probably won't look at you. If you do like an ad agency, you'll get "pitched" for the business by the upper-level business development guys, or agency heads, and then have your project shunted to a junior partner (or, nightmare of nightmares, to a raw rookie who just joined).

Table 1-1. Schedule of Fees for Freelance Publicity

PUBLICITY PROJECT	FEE (IN 1995 DOLLARS)
Booklet	800
Case history	1,000
Consulting	125 per hour
Day rates (per diem) for freelance writing services	750
Feature article	750
Film, slide presentation, or other audiovisual script	100 per minute
Newsletter	250 per page
Press release	300
Speech, 20-minute	2,500

DOING IT YOURSELF

Now you know why I believe so strongly in do-it-yourself type publicity. And why this book is a *must-read* for you. It costs less, you have better control, and you can move faster, since you're the one working the project.

In the next chapter, we'll discuss how to lay the groundwork for your consultancy.

CHAPTER 2

Laying the
Groundwork

Before you build a house, you first must lay the foundation. So it is with publicity for consultants.

Now, while I know you're anxious to get started, if we don't understand the basic components of publicity, it can kill your success.

It would be like trying to put up the framing and roof before laying concrete to hold them up. So indulge me, dear reader, while I explain what publicity is and is not.

PUBLICITY AND ADVERTISING

First, publicity is *not* free advertising. I can't go to the *New York Times* tomorrow and tell them, "I want you to run a story on page one of the metro section all about my consultancy." (Well, I could, but they'd put me away in a straitjacket.) If I did, the paper would likely tell me to "go buy an ad!" And right they'd be to say that.

Advertising is paid-for promotion, be it print ads, commercials, billboards, direct mail, or other media.

Yet I have many students come into my *Getting FREE Publicity* course at various community colleges in California looking for ways to get "free advertising." No such thing, folks.

Second, publicity is *not* something the press or media owes you just because you're in business or you're a "consultant."

Just because you've opened up the greatest management consulting firm in New York City, don't expect the media to care or to jump at the chance to interview the next "guru." You've got to give them a reason. You'll learn how in Chapter 4.

Third, publicity is *not* necessarily something you do in lieu of advertising for your consultancy. In fact, it's something you do in addition to paid-for promotions.

Publicity is a systematic, planned approach to gaining access to the media through the use of good story ideas, good relationship building, and good communication skills. In other words, it's about communicating the *right words* to the *right people* about the *right subject* at the *right time*.

PUBLICITY AND PUBLIC RELATIONS

Public relations and publicity are not the same, though many people make the mistake of calling the process by either name.

Public relations is the total communications program you'll use to reach the various "publics" you need to deal with—potential clients, communities, the press, other consultants, and so on.

Publicity is using various communication tools and techniques to persuade the media to print or broadcast your story about your company or clients. Good publicity is persuading them to print your story ideas over and over again. What these communication tools are you'll learn in Chapters 5 and 6.

Publicity is a component, albeit a very important one, of public relations. So while we will explore the plans, strategies, and objectives of a good publicity campaign, it's beyond the scope of this book to cover the entire spectrum of a consultant's communication campaign. So we'll stick to the basics of getting your story out fast, easily, and affordably.

PUBLICITY VS. ADVERTISING

To make sure you understand the differences between publicity and advertising, and how each fits in your communication program, I'll illustrate with a balance scale. We'll take the advertising balance scale first.

Figure 2-1 shows a typical balance scale like the ones used in old pharmacies to measure compounds. The scale is balanced since we haven't put anything on it yet.

I want to use the balance to compare three factors—cost, control, and credibility. First, let's examine the cost factor.

Does it cost money to advertise? Must I pay for a full-page ad in the *New York Times* or *The Wall Street Journal?* Of course;

Figure 2-1. Plan balance scale

they don't give space away. So let's put one brass weight on the scale to represent cost.

Second, let's look at control. Do I have some control with my advertising? You bet I do. Since I'm paying for the space or airtime, I can determine when I want to run, how big the ad should be, what the message is, and other factors. And by coordinating these factors, I can, within reason, determine the likely results.

Finally, let's consider credibility. Just how credible is advertising? If you said, "Not very," you're right. People these days are jaded, not likely to believe advertising very much. Then why do it? To push people to make decisions now, when we want them to. Advertising forces people to move, which builds our customer base.

So look at Figure 2-2, the advertising balance scale. Kind of lopsided in favor of control, which is good, and cost, which isn't; as for credibility—very light or not at all!

Now let's look at Figure 2-3, the balance scale for publicity. Notice that it's the opposite of the advertising one. Cost is light (we like that!), credibility is very heavy (outstanding!)—but oh, oh, control is very light. As I said earlier, you can't order any paper or broadcast medium to "run my story on page 1."

How does this relate to your consultancy? Watch!

If the scale for advertising is lopsided one way and the one for publicity is its mirror image, lopsided the exact opposite way, if I put the two together, as in Figure 2-4, the combination balances again as it did in Figure 2-1.

And that's what I want you to do. Prepare a *balanced* marketing plan, using both publicity *and* advertising. As a consultant, you'll use publicity to:

1. Increase awareness of your business and the type of clients you deal with.
2. Enhance your image to your various publics.

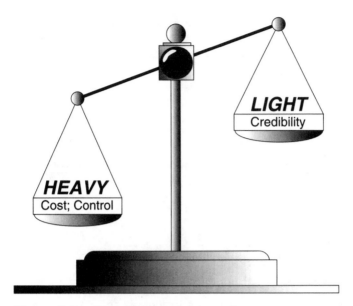

Figure 2-2. Advertising balance scale

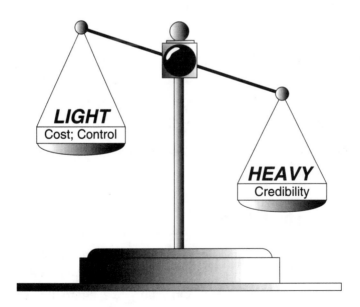

Figure 2-3. Publicity balance scale

11

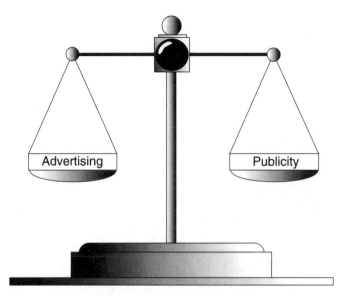

Figure 2-4. Balanced marketing mix scale

    3.   Present yourself as a credible expert.

    4.   Generate *possible* leads.

You'll use advertising to:

    1.   Announce specific offers or benefits to your various audiences.

    2.   Help people make a buying decision now.

    3.   Increase your sales immediately.

By using both, you'll have that balanced communication program most consultants want.

Publicity's Limitations

Notice I said publicity could generate *possible* leads for you. I've never seen, except in rare instances, publicity generate tons of sales of a product or service. Oh, sure, I've heard the story of

Trivial Pursuit too, where they only did publicity and got thousands of orders. But here's the reality:

- They had a concentrated campaign, done very well by pros who knew how.
- It was a national campaign, working through the major press. (As a local consultant, it's not likely you'll find yourself on the pages of *The Wall Street Journal* or on *Oprah*— although it's possible with the right story and persistence.)
- They were there first. It's the old adage: He who gets there first wins the lion's share. So if you're not the first consultant to start a new tradition or come up with a winning way to overcome the national debt, it's unlikely you'll pull many client sales.
- It was product publicity. And that's why this book is different. Product publicity is easier because the public can see it, taste it, feel it, use it. You, on the other hand, deal in intangibles— making business better, helping people get well, reengineering whatever. As consultants we are dealing with feelings and perceptions, not with hard products. Intangibles and feelings are harder to get publicity for.

Turning Straw into Gold

But let me get back to the possible leads—*possible* being the operative word. Whenever a story about me runs and I get any book sales or client inquiries, I consider that gravy. In fact, I really don't expect people to call and offer to hire me from a story.

There is a way for you, however, to turn those media stories, using a publicity-and-advertising combo, into clients. And that's to do what I do.

I make reprints of the story on my letterhead and send copies out to my database of clients and students. (That's paid direct-mail advertising.) The story is, in effect, a third-party endorsement. "See," it says, "Reece is credible. Not because he says so, but because the Podunk paper says so. And everyone reads the Podunk paper, so it must be true."

Then when I telemarket to the client base or send another brochure or flyer (paid advertising, again, by the way), the reprinted story has paved the way for my sales pitch. And I usually pick up two or three clients that way. (You can also use the reprints selectively, sending them out with proposal packets or in an FYI letter.)

Pros and Cons of Publicity

According to Paul and Sarah Edwards, authors of *Getting Business to Come to You,* there are major pros and cons to the use of publicity. The pros we've already talked about—increased credibility, a high profile, access to the right people, and so on.

It's the cons we have to be aware of (though we should not become so scared that we abandon ship before we set sail):

1. *It takes a considerable time investment to create the materials.* That's true. However, with the templates in this book and on disk (supplied with the hardcover edition), it will be much easier.
2. *It takes time to get results.* Yes, you're going to need patience. It may take six months to a year or more before you feel anything (although it shouldn't, if the story angle is sharp and you use the techniques right.)
3. *You must develop and commit to a long-range plan.* True. I can't discipline you and make you pay your dues. Only you can.
4. *It's somewhat out of your control.* Not entirely. There are ways, and there are ways—not manipulative tricks but a set process to make the media your friends, so they do more stories for you than for your competition.

5. *The media use their impression of you, which may differ from the image you have of yourself.* Yup. So make sure the impression you present is positive and authoritative, one of an expert. (More on that later.)
6. *There is a financial investment in press kits, releases, photos, etc.* All true, though not as much as some PR agencies will quote you.
7. *It requires knowledge, skills, and creativity.* Yeah, but I'm going to teach you the knowledge and skills you need. Creativity I can't teach; I can just tell you how to develop it.

OBJECTIVES, STRATEGIES, TACTICS, AND GOALS

Just so you don't get confused, objectives are what you want to happen in your practice—the end result. They are defined in terms of image and client base, over a specific time period. Strategies are how you get there, the what-do-you-do. And for those of you who understand military terminology, tactics are *specifics* based on the strategies. Goals are the time-sequenced ways you measure if you've been successful.

For example, a computer consultant might want to set the following objectives for the year to come:

1. Be positioned as an expert on Novell networking in a two-county area.
2. Increase credibility as an authority for midlevel businesses needing computers.
3. Open doors to better relations with university faculty.
4. Promote high visibility in the business community.

In order to make this clearer to you, here are some objectives you might want to consider when beginning to plan *your* publicity campaign:

1. Be seen in the community as a caring, warm, sharing person.
2. Be seen as the expert in your field in your area of greatest strength.
3. Be called upon whenever anyone has a question about your area of greatest strength.
4. Be the first person who comes to mind whenever anyone thinks about your industry.

Good objectives. Very heady. To show you how this works in real life, we'll use my company as an example. I call my company MarketSmarts. Let's begin to develop a matrix grid (Figure 2-5), which we'll fill out as we go along.

Community: _____ Population: _____	
Objective	
1. Be seen in the community as a caring, warm, sharing person.	
2. Be seen as the expert in publicity in the Inland Empire (the two-county area where I live).	
3. Be called upon whenever anyone has a question about publicity.	
4. Be the first person who comes to mind whenever anyone thinks about consultant publicity.	

Figure 2-5. Objective Matrix

Developing the Strategies

When you first develop the strategies that will move you towards your objectives, don't expect to nail down the specifics of what methods to use right away. That takes time and understanding,

OBJECTIVE	STRATEGY
1. Be seen in the community as a caring, warm, sharing person.	A. Offer free speeches on how to get media attention. B. Offer free consulting to a local charity on publicity for a major fund-raising project.
2. Be seen as the expert in publicity in the Inland Empire (the two-county area where I live).	A. Get placement of stories on my practice in local and regional newspapers on a regular basis. B. Write column on my areas of expertise on a regular basis. C. Give speeches on writing and publicity. D. Give seminars and workshops on writing and publicity. E. Teach community college courses on publicity.
3. Be called upon whenever anyone has a question about publicity.	A. Set up publicity hotline for local corporations with emergencies. B. Do Q-and-A column in a local paper. C. Convert college seminar into cable television show.
4. Be the first person who comes to mind whenever anyone thinks about consultant publicity.	A. Join national and local Public Relations Society of America chapters. Give speeches about consultant publicity. B. Join a national consultant association. Write articles on consultant publicity. Offer seminars. C. Write a book, The Consultant's Guide to Publicity (the one you're now reading). D. Convert book into seminars nationwide for consultants.

Figure 2-6. Objective/Strategy Matrix

17

which you'll get in Chapters 5 and 6. For now, let's just sketch out in general terms how we *might* achieve these objectives. So Figure 2-6 shows what the completed matrix might look like.

A Tactician Be

During the Gulf War, General Schwarzkopf was considered a master tactician. The strategists, President Bush and the Joint Chiefs, decided to strike at Iraq at a certain time (the strategy). The tacticians, led by Schwarzkopf, determined who would strike and when and where the surprise would come (the how). So it is with publicity.

Back to our matrix. Figure 2-7 shows how it looks with tactical implementation.

Setting Goals

Goals are the numerical benchmarks you set for yourself, based on your objectives. For goals to be realistic, they should be short term, measurable, exciting, targeted, and big.

Short Term. There's nothing more frustrating than setting goals that are so distant they don't mean anything. Most people can't realistically plan two or more years out without feeling a sense of frustration that "we'll never make it." People need a sense of accomplishment, and the easiest way to get it is by breaking things down to bite-sized chunks. It's like eating dinner—you don't swallow the entire meal in one big gulp; you eat appetizer first, then the salad, and so on. So it is with goals. A little bit at a time.

Measurable. If you can't measure your goal, how do you know if you've reached it? The best way is to define exactly how to measure it. For example, you would have "Get one publicity story in a local paper per month" rather than "Get visibility in newspapers in California." The latter expression is an objective, not a goal.

OBJECTIVE	STRATEGY	TACTIC
1. Be seen in the community as a caring, warm, sharing person.	A. Offer free speeches on how to get media attention.	Contact Chamber of Commerce, City of Chino, City of Chino Hills, Rotary, Kiwanis, Lions, Elks.
	B. Offer free consulting to a local charity on publicity for a major fund-raising project.	Contact Chino YMCA, House of Ruth, or Kids Shelter.
2. Be seen as the expert in publicity in the Inland Empire (the two-county area where I live).	A. Get placement of stories on my practice in local and regional newspapers on a regular basis.	Contact *Chino Champion, Daily Bulletin.*
	B. Write column on my areas of expertise on a regular basis.	Same as 2A above.
	C. Give speeches on writing and publicity.	Contact Women in Business, Chamber, Small Bus. Devel.
	D. Give seminars and workshops on writing and publicity.	Same as 2C above.
	E. Teach community college courses on publicity.	Contact Chaffey College, Mt. Sac, CSSB.
3. Be called upon whenever anyone has a question about publicity.	A. Set up publicity hotline for local corporations with emergencies.	Contact GTE.
	B. Do Q-and-A column in a local paper.	Write six sample columns; submit to list in 2A.
	C. Convert college seminar into cable television show.	Contact Chino Valley Cable; write outline; video seminar; show to cable station.

Figure 2-7. Objective/Strategy/Tactic Matrix (continued on next page)

OBJECTIVE	STRATEGY	TACTIC
4. Whenever anyone thinks about consultant publicity, they automatically think about me.	A. Join national and local PRSA chapters. Give speeches about consultant publicity.	Get *Directory of Associations;* find address; call for membership applications; join; begin to develop rapport; offer free speeches.
	B. Join a national consultant association. Write articles on consultant publicity. Offer seminars.	Same as 4A above.
	C. Write a book, *The Consultant's Guide to Publicity* (the one you're now reading).	Write outline and proposal; get list of business book publishers; send query letters; follow up with phone calls.
	D. Convert book into seminars nationwide for consultants.	Give completed manuscript to typist/secretary to revamp into outline format; make description and one-page outline into four-page brochure; find mailing list of consultants; send direct-mail piece.

Figure 2-7. (Continued)

Exciting. Without exciting goals, you won't be motivated to do anything towards your objectives. But exciting for one consultant may be boring for another. I remember the first publicity story I ever got. Boy, was I excited! A two-column story on my helping out with the 1972 Democratic Telethon in my hometown of Chicago. I still get excited thinking about it. The *Chicago Tribune,* big city newspaper.

Yet other consultants, who regularly are quoted in *The Wall Street Journal,* might consider that passé. And to me, a story in my hometown newspaper, while initially thrilling, no longer makes me jump up and down. I've progressed beyond that. The point is, what excites you depends on your experience.

A word of caution: Just because you're not hitting the big kahunas, like the *New York Times* or *The Wall Street Journal,* don't think it isn't exciting if you're in your local paper. If you land a regular weekly column in your city pub, that is definitely exciting—and beneficial to your practice.

Targeted.   This is the most important quality for a goal. You can't be all things to all people. Ergo, you can't set goals to be in every publication in your state or the nation, all at one time. First, it's not realistic. Second, too much time and money are involved. Third, it just won't happen. Remember, the press determines when and where your story goes, not you. So design your program with a specific target audience in mind. (We'll discuss targeting media in depth in Chapter 7.)

Big.   While I said we want to set goals in bite-sized chunks, if they're not big enough to make you stretch, you won't do anything. Don't make them impossible to reach within a given time period, but don't make them too easy either.

Let's finish with our Objective/Strategy/Tactic matrix by adding specific timelines—see Figure 2-8. (Those of you familiar with project management software or PERT charts can convert the matrix very easily.)

Now it's your turn. Fill in the blanks in Figure 2-9 for your particular consulting practice.

OBJECTIVE	STRATEGY	TACTIC	TIMELINE
1. Be seen in the community as a caring, warm, sharing person.	A. Offer free speeches on how to get media attention.	Contact Chamber of Commerce, City of Chino, City of Chino Hills, Rotary, Kiwanis, Lions, Elks.	Within 2 years.
	B. Offer free consulting to a local charity on publicity for a major fund-raising project.	Contact Chino YMCA, House of Ruth, or Kids Shelter.	
2. Be seen as the expert in publicity in the Inland Empire (the two-county area where I live).	A. Get placement of stories on my practice in local and regional newspapers on a regular basis.	Contact *Chino Champion*, *Daily Bulletin*.	Within 3 years.
	B. Write column on my areas of expertise on a regular basis.	Same as 2A above.	
	C. Give speeches on writing and publicity.	Contact Women in Business, Chamber, Small Bus. Devel.	
	D. Give seminars and workshops on writing and publicity.	Same as 2C above.	
	E. Teach community college courses on publicity.	Contact Chaffey College, Mt. Sac, CSSB.	

Figure 2-8. Objective/Strategy/Tactic/Timeline Matrix

Goal	Action Steps	Method	Timeframe
3. Be called upon whenever anyone has a question about publicity.	A. Set up publicity hotline for local corporations with emergencies.	Contact GTE.	Within 1 year.
	B. Do Q-and-A column in a local paper.	Write 6 sample columns; submit to list in 2A.	
	C. Convert college seminar into cable television show.	Contact Chino Valley Cable; write outline; video seminar; show to cable station.	
4. Be the first person who comes to mind whenever anyone thinks about consultant publicity.	A. Join national and local PRSA chapters. Give speeches about consultant publicity.	Get *Directory of Associations*; find address; call for membership applications; join; begin to develop rapport; offer free speeches.	Within 2 years.
	B. Join a national consultant association. Write articles on consultant publicity. Offer seminars.	Same as 4A above.	
	C. Write book, *The Consultant's Guide to Publicity* (the one you're now reading).	Write outline and proposal; get list of business book publishers; send query letters; follow up with phone calls.	
	D. Convert book into seminars nationwide for consultants.	Give completed manuscript to typist/secretary to revamp into outline format; make description and one-page outline into four-page brochure; find mailing list of consultants; send direct-mail piece.	

Figure 2-8. (Continued)

Community _____ Population _____

OBJECTIVE	STRATEGY	TACTIC	TIMELINE

Figure 2-9. Your Objective/Strategy/Tactic/Timeline Matrix

Summary

It should be obvious that filling out these charts takes time and knowledge. While you have the time, you haven't been given the knowledge yet to fill out the tactical part. That comes in Chapter 3, "Developing a Publicity Plan."

CHAPTER 3

Developing a Publicity Plan

Many consultants ask me why they should develop a specific publicity-campaign plan. As stated in Chapter 1, the consultant who doesn't plan his own promotion and exposure is like the one who doesn't plan his client's projects—he's an out-of-work (or soon-to-be) practitioner.

On the other hand, sometimes consultants plan too much. They get so caught up in the research and what they're going to do that they never get down to doing it. This chapter will give you the nuts and bolts of the planning process, so you can follow step 1, then do step 2, and so on. Easy, simple, fast.

While we've already talked about objectives, strategies, goals, and tactics in terms of setting a foundation, we need to address the entire planning process, in order to see how they fit into the big picture.

THE PROCESS, THE APPROACH, THE RESEARCH

Process means the exact steps you'll take to determine what to do when. It involves determining your best target audiences, learning where they find out about you, and targeting those specific media that can give you the most bang for the buck.

Approach involves the direction you intend to take in contacting your target-audience media, be it decided by geographic area, demographic characteristic, or both. The approach you use will determine the content of your press release, and other specific publicity tools.

For example, if you were approaching a campaign geographically, you'd start with your local newspapers and radio stations. It wouldn't make sense, therefore, to write a release talking about the magnificent work you've done for a certain client in Podunk, Massachusetts, if your local paper were in Southern California. The editors at your local paper simply wouldn't be interested.

Similarly, if your main audience involved Fortune 500 clients, you wouldn't necessarily target local or regional newspapers since the CEOs you would be trying to reach look for consulting help in major business periodicals and journals.

Research is using the appropriate media and association directories and, depending on the approach you've decided on, culling through them to find the best target media for your particular campaign.

To show how process, approach, and research work together, let's walk through a real-world example: Say you're a financial consultant working in a small midwestern town of around 100,000 population. You want people to know how great you are and how you can help them with their estate, retirement, and general financial planning.

The Process

Step 1: Decide which of the three areas you specialize in—estate, retirement, and general financial planning—has been the most lucrative for you. Look at your past sales figures—which clients bought what service the most. Suppose the majority of them deal in retirement planning. You like doing it, you're good at it, it's comfortable. So, do you do one release on retirement, then move on to estate and general planning?

Answer: no. A publicity campaign needs a theme to be effective, just like an ad campaign. We'll pick retirement as the theme for your first full publicity campaign. Figure 3-1 shows why—retirement planning has been your most lucrative (read profitable) specialty area during the past two years. And it may take between six months to a year before you saturate the market. That's why you're publicizing this specialty first.

OK, so it's retirement. That's the first part of the process—we've determined your best target audience for a publicity campaign—people who need retirement planning.

Step 2: Find out where the people in your target audience (your potential clients) normally look for retirement information. If they're part of a large corporation that has a retirement plan, I suppose the company has a retirement specialist. And that specialist *may* offer the newsletter editor at the plant a retirement column. (Most big corporations have internal newsletters, a much overlooked source for great publicity.)

However, you can be the big hero. You see, most newsletter editors at major companies do that task as part-time work. They're normally the human resources or marketing communications specialist

	HOW MANY CLIENTS?	
My Specialties	This Year	Last Year
Estate planning	27	15
Retirement planning	110	77
General financial planning	58	33

Figure 3-1. Developing a Publicity Plan

at the plant. And they don't have the time. But they've got to do it—it's an order from the boss.

Here you come, a bona fide retirement specialist, offering to do a FREE article once a month on retirement problems and solutions. Do you think if you offer this the newsletter editor, or slave, will welcome your article with open arms?

You bet! I know several corporate, part-time newsletter editors. They hate it. Whenever I offer a column, they jump at the chance to use it. "And oh, by the way, I happen to have six articles, a series, already produced for you to insert . . . is that OK?" What do you think their response is? If you said like seeing an angel from heaven, you'd be close. They love me. And they'll love you too. It's a win-win: They get articles they don't have to sweat over; you get FREE Publicity. Just make sure your name and phone number are at the bottom of your copy. (More about that in Chapter 5, on writing easy articles.)

Now, where else do people look for retirement info? The local paper? Perhaps. Can you offer your local rag the same series of six articles, but tailored to the community, with local examples of real clients you've helped? Of course!

How about association publications? Yes, if you belong to the association. If you don't, it may be harder to get articles published by them.

Then there are senior citizen magazines and newspapers, senior centers, accountants who tell their clients to put money away for retirement, and other sources of retirement info. Let's make a list (Table 3-1) to begin to see where we can find viable targets that might have accessible media we could tap into.

Step 3: Now that we have a rough (by no means comprehensive) idea of where we can find our audience, we need to fill in answers to what types of media these people would use to gather info about retirement. Let's go back to our list and fill it in (see Table 3-2). After that we'll be ready to scope out our approach.

Table 3-1. Contacting Target Audiences for Retirement Planning

Target Audience Info Channel	Possible Media
Corporations	
Work in general	
Associations	
Senior centers	
Accountants	
Chambers of Commerce	
Unions	
Newspapers	
Magazines	
Radio shows	
Television shows	
Friends	

The Approach

Ask yourself whether you want to approach your target audience geographically, demographically, or both. The factors to consider include your past client history, whether you've really saturated your local area, and how much you're capable of doing outside your own area without straining yourself and your resources.

If you want to target your audience geographically, pick the area you intend to saturate with your publicity campaign, and analyze what the target audience would read in that area.

If you want to go demographically, determine your audience profile, and assess which media they would use. (Demographics, by the way, are those nice profile types the census bureau calculates every ten years, like age, income, sex, households, etc.)

You can combine a geographic campaign and a demographic campaign; this gives the best results. For example, if you're a local consultant catering to retirement planners within a ten-mile radius,

Table 3-2. Contacting Target Audiences for Retirement Planning, with Media Identified

Target Audience Info Channel	Possible Media
Corporations	Employee newsletters, corporate magazines, executive magazines
Work in general	Too broad; can't define
Associations	Association newsletters, conventions
Senior centers	Possible newsletters; senior mags
Accountants	Society publications
Chambers of Commerce	Newsletters
Unions	Newsletters
Newspapers	Local, regional
Magazines	Targeted to retirement audiences
Radio shows	Targeted to retirement audiences
Television shows	Targeted to retirement audiences
Friends	Word-of-mouth

you may want to rethink your target demographics within the local area. Have you really tapped all those in your area who don't have retirement plans? I doubt it.

So, if the majority of your past clients have been between the ages of 35 and 54, that is the target age range you want. Then add income level and other factors to flesh out your profile. Now we add these additional factors to our grid to determine exactly who we should target—see Figure 3-2. We finish the grid with an action list. Then we're ready to do some research.

The Research

The research part comes here, where you determine specifically where you will send your press announcements (or whatever publicity tools you're going to use). The first step is to acquaint yourself

Profile Category	Profile Specifics
Client demographics	Age 35–54, two-income home, $100,000+ total combined income, kids age 12 and up
Client geographic area	10-mile radius around office; includes cities of Covina, San Dimas, La Verne, Upland, Chino, Chino Hills, Ontario, Pomona, Corona, Montclair, Diamond Bar, and Claremont
Best target audience	Retirement planning (geographic campaign)

Client Contact Channel	Possible Media	Action
Corporations	Employee newsletters, corporate magazines, executive magazines	Check industrial directories; *Oxbridge Direct. of Newsletters*
Associations	Association newsletters, conventions	Check Encyclopedia of Assocs.
Senior centers	Possible newsletters; senior mags	Check Area on Aging local office
Accountants	Society publications	Check Directories in Print
Chambers of Commerce	Newsletters	Contact all chambers per city
Unions	Newsletters	Check associations' directories
Newspapers	Local, regional	Check media guides
Magazines	Targeted to retirement audiences	Check media guides
Radio shows	Targeted to retirement audiences	Check media guides
Television shows	Targeted to retirement audiences	Check media guides

Figure 3-2. Client Profile

with the various media directories available, so you can put together a media contact file. (For a complete description, see Chapter 5.)

Once you've put your list together, get copies of the publications to see if they're right for your target audience profile. Ask for a media kit, which will include reader profiles, rate cards, and other

31

promotional materials. You want the reader profile, which says what type of person reads a particular publication. If they match your audience profile, use them. If not, stay away (unless you're doing a specific geographic area only).

Table 3-3 shows how the grid looks after research has turned the action list of Figure 3-2 into added contact categories.

The Publicity-Project Tracking Sheet

In my publicity classes, I offer students a simplified publicity-project tracking sheet to help them outline what we've discussed above. Figure 3-3 shows an easy version you can use in your consulting practice.

SETTING GOALS

In setting your goals and objectives (see Chapter 1), it's important to determine exactly what you want to achieve and make sure

Table 3-3. Information Sources

TARGET GROUP	INFORMATION SOURCE
Corporations	Southern Cal. industrial dir. list (on cards)
Associations	Area on Aging—So. Cal. office
Senior centers	All cities
Accountants	AICPA, CSEA, CSCPA
Chambers of Commerce (all chambers per city)	All have newsletters
Unions	List of unions in area
Newspapers	*Champion Publications; Inland Daily Bulletin, Claremont Courier, Inland Business Journal, San Dimas Express, San Gabriel Valley Tribune, San Bernardino County Sun, Corona-Norco Independent*
Magazines	Check media guides
Radio shows	*Sunday Senior,* KVFM
Television shows	KABC, KNBC, KCBS, KESQ

PROJECT: _____

DUE DATE: _____

GOALS SET: _____

WHO DO WE WANT TO REACH? _____

WHY DO WE WANT TO REACH THEM? _____

MEDIA ANALYSIS:

  THEY MIGHT READ: _____

  THEY MIGHT WATCH: _____

  THEY MIGHT LISTEN TO: _____

APPROACH:

  GEOGRAPHICALLY _____

  DEMOGRAPHICALLY _____

RESEARCH:

  BACON'S _____

  WORKING PRESS _____

  GALE DIRECTORY _____

  STD. RATE & DATA _____

  READER'S GUIDE _____

SELECTION:

  MAGAZINES _____

  NEWSPAPERS _____

  RADIO _____

  TV _____

OBTAIN SAMPLES:

MAGAZINES/NEWSPAPERS/RADIO/TELEVISION (3 OF EACH)—FOCUS ON:

  STYLE _____

  PHILOSOPHY _____

REPORTERS _____

WRITE IT ALL DOWN
PREPARE THE NEWS RELEASE
SEND THE NEWS RELEASE
TRACK THE RESULTS

Figure 3-3. A publicity project tracking sheet

everything you do in terms of publicity relates to those specific goals. If something seems nice or has a "wouldn't it be great if we could be on *Oprah?*" ring to it but will do nothing to help you reach your goals and objectives, abandon immediately.

In fact, you might want to write a short mission statement that specifically defines who you are, who you target, and how you intend to get there. Using the example from Chapter 1, a mission statement for the computer consultant might read:

> The purpose of XYZ Computer Consulting is to sell and service the small-business market [defined demographic target] of San Diego County [defined geographic target] the finest quality computer-networking hardware and software. We intend to position ourselves as a leading expert on Novell networking products and as an authority for midlevel businesses needing computers. We intend to promote this position by (1) generating high visibility in the business community, (2) improving relations with university computer faculty, and (3) constantly re-educating and upgrading our skill levels. (rewrite of the objectives)

Why rewrite your Chapter 2 goals and objectives in one simple paragraph that adds the targets? So it's clear to you and everyone you touch. Your mission is your message. If you can't communicate it clearly to yourself, let alone to others, you don't have a handle on it. And you can't write up your plan.

Reaching Your Targets

Obviously, the first step in goal setting is determining who your target audiences are. In the example above, we determined for a financial consultant that his targets, based on his previous client history, would be individuals or couples who had a need for retirement planning, general financial planning, and estate planning. Since the majority of his previous customers came for retirement, that became his first target.

What about you? Can you figure out who your best audiences are so you know how to develop a publicity campaign that reaches more of them? Use Table 3-4 to set up a target market "hit list."

Notice that I have included a third column in Table 3-4, "Average Billing per Year." The reason—I earlier told you to determine your best target by profitability. Suppose you had 11 clients each billing $2,000 per year, and 44 clients each billing $500 per year, and both groups were involved in general financial planning. Which one would you target first? If you said the 11 at $2,000, you'd be wrong. Why? Both gross $22,000, right? Yet, if you lose one of the 11 you're $2,000 down. If you lose one of the 44, you're down only $500—not such a big hit. I know, you'd rather have all big fish. But when it comes to losses and the types of clients publicity can generate, the conservative approach is best. (By the way, I'm not saying ignore the target audience of the

Table 3-4. Target Market Hit List

PAST CLIENT TYPES	NUMBER OF CLIENTS	AVG. BILLING PER YEAR

big kahunas; just put it second instead of first on the list for a publicity campaign. And you may even get some big ones from the campaign devoted to the midsized guys.)

How Many Targets at Once?

The number of target audiences you try to reach in a single campaign depends on your budget and your timeline. There's no such thing as a typical publicity budget because it's the strategies and tactics you use that determine how much to spend, not the other way around. In this respect a publicity budget is just like a marketing budget. My students always ask me, "How much should I spend?" My answer is, "Why ask me? Ask your prospects!" Whatever methods or media they tell you they use to find out about you, that's where, in your specific geographic areas, you put your money.

Publicity Budgeting

In the old days, before somebody got smart, there were many catch-as-catch-can methods for publicity budgeting. The first was *percentage of sales*. This tells you to set aside a certain percentage of your gross sales. The problem: publicity is long term, and its results cannot be measured as fast as the results of direct-response advertising can. So you spent your percentage and waited . . . and waited . . . and waited—sort of like the you-know-who bunny.

Nor does this account for seasonality (yes, there are seasons in publicity, as in advertising)—for peaks and valleys. And it doesn't consider the competition, either.

The second old method, *last year's publicity budget plus a certain percentage,* is also wrong. Costs go up every year. This method doesn't consider inflation, cost of goods sold, or anything else.

Methods 3 and 4, *match the competition* and *all you can afford,* are basically throwing your money down the sewer. How do you know if your competition is really getting results? You don't. They may have an insider at a paper (not a necessity for getting publicity, but a definite help) or have a freelance writer working with them. *All you can afford* is the mud-on-the-wall theory of budgeting.

Listen, if you're going to do this type of budgeting, I have a suggestion: Write out a blank check in the amount you plan to spend and send it to me. I'll pass it on to my favorite charity. It'll do more good there than it will for you.

The only real, sane way to budget is by the *objective and task method*. It simply states what our objectives are (see Chapter 1 if you forget), what the tasks (strategies and tactics) are that we have to implement to fulfill those objectives, and what the cost will be over a one-year period (the minimum amount of time you should devote to a publicity campaign) (see Figure 3-4).

ONE YEAR MINIMUM

OBJECTIVE	TASK (STRATEGY/TACTIC)	COST

Figure 3-4.   Objective/Task Budget Form

DEVELOPING A PUBLICITY PLAN

NAME _____

PART 1. SELF-DESCRIPTION

PRESENT   What are you now? _____

_____

PAST   What are your major achievements? _____

_____

FUTURE   What are your plans and dreams?_____

_____

GOAL   How do you want to be known?_____

_____

PART 2. PRIMARY FACTS

1   How do you like to spend your time? _____

_____

2   Name any unusual hobbies. _____

_____

3   Are you the mate, ex-mate, or relative of someone famous?_____

_____

4   What would you like to do in the distant future? _____

_____

5   Do you have any secret ambitions? _____

_____

6   What don't you like about your community? _____

_____

7   What are some things you don't like about the world? _____

_____

8   What is your ancestry and religion? _____

_____

Fig. 3-5.   A personality profile form

NAME   John and Jane Doe of Los Angeles, CA

PART 1. SELF-DESCRIPTION

PRESENT	What are you now?	Jr. Vice Pres., Consultant, IBM (John) Vice President, Midwest Bank (Jane)
PAST	What are your major achievements?	First system designers for Kmart Mainframes; Project consultants for Porsche, North America; Founders, Independent Computer Consultants Assn. (ICCA); Founders, Computer Museum of America
FUTURE	What are your plans and dreams?	Start a computer school for under-privileged kids; build own consulting business to self-sufficiency
GOAL	How do you want to be known?	Known nationally as leading computer consultants

PART 2. PRIMARY FACTS

1	How do you like to spend your time?	Not much spare time, but like to have friends over; visit antique stores; visit art museums
2	Name any unusual hobbies.	We own a small antique store in Del Mar, CA. We have an unusual antique collection and collect Erté art
3	Are you the mate, exmate, or relative of someone famous?	No
4	What would you like to do in the distant future?	Retire to the mountains near Reno; fish; enjoy life
5	Do you have any secret ambitions?	No
6	What don't you like about your community?	We live in suburban Los Angeles. Far too crowded. Not safe to go out at night
7	What are some things you don't like about the world?	People don't seem to respect consultants. Anyone can hang up a shingle and call themselves one. Too much population and pollution on the planet.
8	What is your ancestry and religion?	Scottish; Presbyterian

Figure 3-6.   Personality profile for computer consultants

GOAL:
ONE
STORY/
MO.

As for a time line, I suggest you set a realistic goal of at least one story on your consultancy per month. That's not too hard. After several have hit, you'll find there's a snowball effect. Then up the quota to two per month, then more. My friend Dr. Jeffrey Lant, author of many publicity and marketing books, set as his goal many years ago to get one story per week. Pretty heady, you say? Well, I'm not sure that he makes it every week, but I do know he's quoted more often than many in the business world. And if he misses a week, he takes that goal and adds it on to the next.

YOUR PUBLICITY PROFILE

We've discussed target audience profiles in depth. Yet most consultants—and others, for that matter—who do publicity fail to define a profile for themselves. This leads to meandering writing when it comes time to put pen to paper or fingers to keyboard. A big stumbling block for most people is "What do I say about myself that the press will take?" Let's start with a personality profile. Gloria Michels, a fellow Chicagoan and the author of *Making Yourself Famous,* calls it a *celebrity profile.* Since she's done this so well, I'll use her forms here. Figure 3-5 is her blank personality profile.

OK, now let's fill out the personality profile for our fictitious computer consultant (see Figure 3-6). I'll base it on a real example, friends of mine from Los Angeles. He's currently an IBM consultant; she's an MIS director for a major bank chain.

John's dream of opening a computer school for underprivileged kids fits right into his comments about suburban Los Angeles. And since he started the ICCA San Diego chapter, he has a background in getting things done. We'll use this, as well as his other qualifications (Kmart, Porsche) to come up with some great story ideas in the next chapter.

CHAPTER 4

Developing Good Story Ideas

WHERE DO GOOD STORY IDEAS COME FROM?

Most consultants, and other business people as well, have a hard time coming up with story ideas that they feel the press will accept. As a writer and publicist, I suppose it's easy for me. There seem to be more ideas out there than I have time to write about. However, you've never done this before. I understand that. To make it easy for you, follow the basic guidelines that I give in this chapter.

There are three ways that you, as a consultant, can get story ideas that will SELL YOU.

1. Use the publicity profile we created in the last chapter;
2. Write about your clients; and
3. Gather ideas from the media (always a good idea to stay fresh).

The secret to finding ideas that will sell your clients and, ultimately, your consulting to the media is to look around you at work or home. Writing about the familiar makes it comfortable, and when you are comfortable, you create and write better.

YOUR CLIENTS FIRST

Let's first cover story ideas about your clients. Why them first and not *your* profile? Because the word *consultant* can have a bad ring to it for media people. In interviewing my friend Jan Norman, small-business reporter at the *Orange County Register,* for this book, I asked if *consultant* is an anathema to most editors and writers. "Not to me," she said, "since I deal with small business and most of my ideas for stories are fed by consultants. However, other reporters I know on the general-assignment desks around Los Angeles loathe the word." In other words, tell a reporter you're a consultant, and you may tap an unexpressed bias that will taint how they write your story—if they write it at all.

Also, it may be easier to get publicity for *yourself* by focusing on your clients. This comes out in another comment Jan made in the interview: Don't call reporters to tell them of the great work you've done again. Instead, tell them about a particular problem a client of yours had and how it was solved. Reporters aren't dumb. They'll get the message that you were the one to solve it without your saying, "And I'm the consultant that did it!" Keep it low key. This has worked well *many* times for me. (See examples in Chapter 7, "Dealing with the Media.")

So, what type of clients have you had in the past? What stories could you write about how you've helped them? What problems might they have in common with other, similar clients who come to you? What does your consultancy do that will make people's lives better? How will it change our world? Why is it better than other consultancies like it? These questions will help you develop ideas on which to base your releases.

Figure 4-1 shows a form that's handy for sorting out answers.

Type of Past Clients, by Industry

Specific Client	How I Helped Them

Competitor Consultancy	Background or Specialty

How Am I Different?

Common Problem or Theme throughout Client History = Good Idea

---

Figure 4-1. A story-generating worksheet to help find the best topics for your publicity releases

Let's fill this worksheet out. We'll use my consultancy as an example since I'm most familiar with it (and, of course, it's a very good example of what works)—see Figure 4-2. After we've filled

Type of Past Clients, by Industry
General small inventors/Backyard and weekend warriors
Mom-and-pop retailers
Service businesses with under 20 employees, in business one to five years
Hospital/Medical physician groups
Industrial manufacturers—plumbing industry, computer industry

Specific Client	How I Helped Them
C. C. Rehab Hospital	Business plan for new project
C. T. Realtor	Market survey/Current analysis
J. M. Company	Publicity for novelty gift
Dentist P. B.	Publicity for dental implant
Consultant R. M.	Local story on career book

Competitor Consultancy	Background or Specialty
T. Stephens	Former DEC product manager
M. Rounds	Former electrical engineer; platform speaker
B. Gaughn	Book publicist
G. Bassine	Direct-mail specialist

How Am I Different?
I focus on small business and inventors with sales under $250,000
Stephens and Rounds only do publicity when they have to
Gaughn is a major threat in the area of book publicity
Bassine is located in Oregon

Common Problem or Theme throughout Client History = Good Idea
Clients don't understand the process of reaching the media (all)
Clients don't know how to write press releases that get results (all)
Collections, retention, upselling to current customers (small business)

Figure 4-2. The story-generating worksheet filled out for the author's consultancy

the worksheet out, we'll take a closer look at its main sections to get a better idea of the hows and whys.

Specific Clients and How I Helped Them

It may be obvious already, but it's worth mentioning that you want to put your "winners" in the client column. When you draw on these client histories to flesh out your news releases and articles, the resulting publicity will showcase you as the expert others are looking for.

Competitor Consultancies—How Am I Different?

I focus on small business and inventors with sales under $250,000. Most publicists don't want to touch those areas. I've developed a niche over the years as the firm who gets high image publicity for business at reasonable cost.

Stephens and Rounds only do publicity when they have to. It's not one of their major themes. In fact, Rounds has called me "one of the best damn writers in the business." Possible use of major competitor's endorsement?

Gaughn is a major threat in the area of book publicity. She has over 20 book clients to her credit; I have three. On the other hand, she's in Santa Barbara and deals with people who pay the big bucks, not with sales under $250,000.

Common Problems Make Good Story Ideas

Have you noticed? The book you are reading is based on discussions of common problems dealing with marketing, advertising, and publicity. And since you've read this far, chances are you too are unsure of how to deal with some (or many) phases of marketing, advertising, and publicity. My clients are looking for a consultant who understands the process of reaching the media and how to develop and write press releases that get results—because they don't.

Following through on this analysis, I'm writing this book by using specific examples of successful client-publicity campaigns and how I did it. This shows you, my readers, the simple steps to take in doing your own publicity. And, in turn, it spreads the word about my expertise in the field.

But what about other kinds of uses? That's where the how-am-I-different analysis comes in. Using it I find I must continue to focus on the little guy and also shy away from book publicity.

Now, I ask, what problems do small-business owners have in common? Probably collections, customer retention, upselling to current customers—the usual. If I do a story on several clients and how I helped solve these common problems, might the press take it? You bet!

What would be the headline? "Local Consultant Sees Upsurge of Collection Problems for Small Business in '95—Gloomy Signs for Economy Predicted." How can I use this admittedly negative headline to showcase me? By looking like a white knight coming to the rescue, of course!

If I decided to use past client history for a story idea, and if I wanted to get more publicity and/or marketing-consulting business from dentists, I'd take Dentist P. B.'s story and weave it into an article, a release, or a short how-to. (You'll learn all these methods in Chapter 6, "Tools of the Trade—Part 2.") Possible headline for a dental trade magazine like *Dental Economics*—"Percentage of Dentists Creating New Products on Rise—Consultant Says Sky's the Limit for Inventor Docs."

Figure 4-3 shows this and other story ideas based on past client history.

Now it's time for *you* to "fill in the blanks." In Figure 4-4, list as many winners as you can. The more story ideas you have, the better your publicity campaign will become. If one idea doesn't work out, go on to the next. By the way, note that the story ideas in Figure 4-3 will work both with a local or regional flavor and with a national scope. It just depends on the media you're targeting.

SPECIFIC CLIENT	HOW I HELPED THEM	POSSIBLE STORY
C. C. Rehab Hospital	Business plan for new project	"Hospitals Find Profit Centers in New Product Rollouts" [Fund-raising]
C. T. Realtor	Market survey/ Current analysis	"Real Estate Survey Shows W-O-M Tops List of Strategies" [Marketing]
J. M. Company	Publicity for novelty gift	"Fads Can *Still* Make You Rich!" [Inventors]
Dentist P. B.	Publicity for dental implant	"Percentage of Dentists Creating New Products on Rise" [Trade PR]
Consultant R. M.	Local story on career book	"Yes, There *Is* Life after Aerospace!"

Figure 4-3. Sample Story Ideas

SPECIFIC CLIENT	HOW I HELPED THEM	POSSIBLE STORY

Figure 4-4. Your Sample Story Ideas

USING THE PUBLICITY PROFILE TO GENERATE IDEAS

Now let's look again at the publicity profile we created in Chapter 3 to determine what other story ideas there may be. As you remember, the profile for the computer consultants appeared as shown in Figure 4-5.

NAME   John and Jane Doe of Los Angeles, CA

PART 1. SELF-DESCRIPTION

PRESENT	What are you now?	Jr. Vice Pres., Consultant, IBM (John) Vice President, Midwest Bank (Jane)
PAST	What are your major achievements?	First system designers for Kmart Mainframes; Project consultants for Porsche, North America; Founders, Independent Computer Consultants Assn. (ICCA); Founders, Computer Museum of America
FUTURE	What are your plans and dreams?	Start a computer school for under-privileged kids; build own consulting business to self-sufficiency
GOAL	How do you want to be known?	Known nationally as leading computer consultants

PART 2. PRIMARY FACTS

1	How do you like to spend your time?	Not much spare time, but like to have friends over; visit antique stores; visit art museums
2	Name any unusual hobbies.	We own a small antique store in Del Mar, CA. We have an unusual antique collection and collect Erté art
3	Are you the mate, exmate, or relative of someone famous?	No
4	What would you like to do in the distant future?	Retire to the mountains near Reno; fish; enjoy life
5	Do you have any secret ambitions?	No
6	What don't you like about your community?	We live in suburban Los Angeles. Far too crowded. Not safe to go out at night
7	What are some things you don't like about the world?	People don't seem to respect consultants. Anyone can hang up a shingle and call themselves one. Too much population and pollution on the planet.
8	What is your ancestry and religion?	Scottish; Presbyterian

Figure 4-5. Personality profile for fictitious computer consultants (Figure 3.6)

Putting the information in Figure 4-5 into a grid like Figures 4-3 and 4-4, we come up with the ideas shown in Figure 4-6. (Since Figure 4-6 is not a real-life example, it omits the "What I Did for Them" column.) These ideas are not all-inclusive; I'm sure you have your own slant or angle on this.

DESCRIPTION/PRIMARY FACT	POSSIBLE STORY IDEAS
First system designers for Kmart Mainframes	How small business can compete with the big boys by using computers (regl., natl. small-biz mags)
Project consultants for Porsche, North America	Using computers to keep track of dealer info (trade mags)
Founders, Independent Computer Consultants Assn.	Donate time to start small-business-consultants group—referrals (shows credibility)
Founders, Computer Museum of America	Offer scholarship to inner-city kids on computer ed.
Spare time: visit antique stores, visit art museums	Donate antique to City Hall—shows community goodwill
Hobbies: unusual antique collection, collect Erté art	Article on keeping collections and art trackable on computer; could lead to speeches
Relative of someone famous	Does not apply
Retire to the mountains near Reno; fish; enjoy life	How to computerize your fishing tackle, info (sports magazines—local, national)
Suburban Los Angeles far too crowded; not safe to go out at night	Start computer school for underprivileged kids in Los Angeles (great angle)
People don't seem to respect consultants	Series—how to pick the right consultant (computer, etc.)
Too much population and pollution on the planet	Using computers to chart population/pollution problems—finding answers
Scottish; Presbyterian	Setting up genealogy on PCs

Figure 4-6. Story-Idea Grid

GATHERING IDEAS FROM THE MEDIA

As I said earlier, it's a good idea to keep abreast of what's happening in the media in terms of story ideas. What the press likes is what they're currently reporting on. So, if you can tie what *you* do into what the press is talking about, you should have it easier in selling them your story angles.

Here's how it works.

Let's start by looking at a newspaper. We'll take today's, which happens to be a Sunday paper. The headline of my local paper says "Haiti Invasion Called Likely." What kind of story ideas, or angles, can you get from this?

If you're a consultant who specializes in multicultural diversity or affirmative action (like one of my clients), the connections are obvious. Put together a release using the facts you know about immigration and the headline story's impact on the U.S. economy; then tie it in with multicultural diversity and affirmative action. Take either the negative approach—"Consultant Says Haiti Invasion Could Jeopardize Affirmative Action Plans in California"—or the positive—"Consultant Says Haiti Immigration to Spur Further Growth of A.A."

If you're a consultant in another discipline, could the Haiti story tie in to what you do? Possibly. Suppose we go back to our computer-consultant example. John and Jane Doe could write about how all the immigration officials cannot keep up with the massive influx of refugees because their computer systems are too antiquated. They could explain what they think the ideal system would be—one that they just happen to sell.

You can do the same with magazines as well. Find magazines that deal with your area of discipline. Look for current-trend articles, astonishing facts, and great stories. Take the basic facts and add your own stories from clients you've had. Then submit them as news releases to local and regional papers. Chances are the reporters haven't read the articles you've drawn on from your industry journals. They're too busy. Just make sure you don't plagiarize the wording. Take the concept.

Electronic, or broadcast, media might offer ideas for your releases also. Watch the *local* evening news during the last ten minutes of the broadcast—that's when stations air their local news "good guy" stories. See what they like to report on. It should load you up with ideas.

The creative consultant keeps an idea book for publicity with them at all times. Add a tape recorder for the car (I get some of my best ideas while driving), and you should have no trouble coming up with angles.

WHAT'S A GOOD STORY IDEA?

OK, you've come up with, say, a dozen or more story ideas that you *think* will work and get you coverage in the press. But how do you know for sure? After all, you just can't copy articles verbatim from newspapers and magazines and put your own byline on them. (A byline is where your name goes on the story, after the headline—"10 Great Story Ideas for Consultants" by Reece Franklin.)

And one reporter's concept of a good story may look like garbage to the next one. In that case it's no go, no sale, and no coverage for your consultancy.

There are four criteria that will determine if your story idea has merit enough to catch the eye of an editor or reporter:

1. Timeliness.
2. The news factor.
3. Human interest.
4. Correct procedures.

Timeliness

The timing of sending in your news release or story idea, and also of when you hold your news event, is crucial to your success. More stories have been lost because of bad timing and missed deadlines than any other reason. So know your deadlines.

If you send in a news release two days before you intend to hold a press conference or event, don't expect the media to get all excited and jump up and down. In fact, unless the electronic media are having a slow news day, your release will be relegated to the "round file."

I recommend the following time lines for sending in a news release (articles have a much longer lead time):

- Daily newspaper or metro—two weeks minimum;
- Weekly or biweekly paper—three weeks minimum;
- Monthly magazines—up to three months (see *Writer's Market* for specifics).

The News Factor

For a story to make the press, it must have what we editors call *newsworthiness*. Exactly what is this? I've asked dozens of fellow newspaper owners, editors, and reporters, and I've gotten the same answer from all of them: There's no hard-and-fast definition.

So much for expert opinion. My advice is to study the newspapers you want to have cover your consultancy. What do they consider news? Same thing with electronic media. You want to be on *Oprah?* You'd darn well better watch *Oprah,* then.

The closest I can come to telling you if your story has news in it is to ask you to give it what I call the *fire-alarm test.*

- Is it urgent—will the media give it a four-alarmer that *has to run?*
- Is it a three-alarm—not as urgent but still very important?
- Is it a two-alarm—interesting but not critical enough to run today or tomorrow?
- Is it just filler—can it run today or tomorrow or next month? That may not even be a one-alarm story.

To you, the story may be a barn burner; to the press, ho–hum. I suggest you show it to people you don't know as well as to some of your associates and clients. If the attitude is "That's interesting," you've got a one-alarmer. If they shout, "Wow!" you've probably got a barn burner.

To explain even further, consider the difference between what the press calls *hard news* and *soft news*. Hard news is what the media MUST report—a fire, tornado, explosion, or political event. Soft news is what they normally get from us consultants—our releases, company-expansion plans, and so on. (That's why you *must* find the angle that will make them sit up and take notice.) The more you can make your soft news sound like hard news, the easier it will be to get it in the media.

Again, read the newspapers, and watch and listen to the talk shows. See what they're reporting on now. If you can figure out how to capitalize on their stories without being blatant, you've got a better chance.

For example, in the computer consultant's situation, since underprivileged kids and gangs are constantly in the news, anything that helps these folks out is bound to be newsworthy. So what if they only reported that you're a computer consultant for three seconds? They said it, didn't they? Sometimes it's better to get coverage without being too self-serving. It goes farther.

Human Interest

The third criterion for a good news story is its human interest. Readers, viewers, and listeners are human beings, and editors and news directors look for stories with the humanity aspect. Put humanity into your publicity, and you'll come out a winner. Human interest is the name of the game.

Take, for example, any charity for children. Since most news stories focus on the negative, any story on desperate or downtrodden children will be grist for the mill. Now, add how you've started that scholarship program to help local kids learn entrepreneurship, and you've got yourself a hook, or story angle.

I always recommend that consultants tie in with a major charity, especially one that has a "news hog" factor, like a health charity. The Muscular Dystrophy Association, Heart Association, and Juvenile Diabetes Foundation come to mind. The media eat that stuff up.

Offer volunteer hours—or better yet, your specific skills—and you've got a sure bet. Our computer-consultant friend offered the local YMCA several old computers and fixed them up so the kids could learn. Instant story, instant coverage, instant credibility.

What's his secret, if many other consultants are doing the same? He lets the charity put out the release. They're so much better at it than he is, and they often have a direct pipeline to or relationship with the local editor.

Correct Procedures

The last of the four criteria is to pay attention to the correct procedures for turning in your ideas and dealing with the media. These include timing, deadlines, writing the release correctly, and handling the press.

Wrong procedures can kill a story, especially when they show that someone hasn't done their homework. For example, the biggest pet peeve editors, reporters, assignment editors (TV), and talk-show producers have is when someone pitches (tries to sell) them on a story and runs off at the mouth, on and on, without knowing what the show or publication is about. Yet the person is *sure* their story idea is "exactly what you're looking for!" Give me a break!

The media live by specific forms and protocols. Knowing these, you're certain to leverage your chances for getting free publicity. (For specifics, see Chapter 7, "Dealing with the Media.")

CHAPTER 5

Tools of the Trade— Releases, Press Kits, Content Files

Of all of the tools of the publicity trade at your disposal, one of the most important is something you design yourself—the media contact file. The media contact file is your gold mine. It's what separates the wheat from the chaff, the men and women from the children.

Without my media contact file, I'd be lost. It's taken me years to develop it, hone it, refine it. It includes all those media mavens I deal with *every* day—the editors, reporters, assignment planners, talk-show producers, and other gatekeepers to the domain of the great, all-powerful print and broadcast media. Without them, I cannot gain entry. Without them, I cannot ply my trade.

And without them, *you* cannot hope to achieve any publicity at all.

It's therefore *IMPERATIVE* (get the point?) that you begin to put together, immediately, your own contact file. People that you'll develop a long-lasting relationship with. So that when they need a quote for a story, they call you, their RESIDENT EXPERT on whatever area of consulting you have expertise in.

For each separate media entity, be it newspaper, magazine, radio news, TV news, or talk show, you'll have a separate index card. (You can do this on a computer, using a contact manager or database. In fact, I have both—a computer database of contacts, *and* the same info on cards. Reason? I've seen that scary phrase too many times on my screen: "File Not Found." Arghh!)

On the back of each card, keep good notes of your conversations with the contact. Over several months you'll see a patterned increase in your contacts and your relationships. Pretty soon you'll "red flag" that card—on the day you become that media's resident expert, their main source for info on a particular subject. That's the day you break out the champagne.

SETTING UP YOUR CARD FILE

Another reason I like to keep an organized card system—it's easier to grab a stack of cards for, say, National Newspapers and follow them up with phone calls after having sent out a release. If contacts were not organized a certain way, I'd have to wade through hundreds of cards to find the ones I wanted to call.

Figure 5-1 shows how to set up your system. I recommend divided tabs put into a 4 × 6 or 5 × 8 card box. (It's set up the same way *most* media directories allocate their sections).

Why do I list radio and TV talk shows as separate categories, instead of under Radio and TV Contacts? The contacts for Radio and Television are for the news departments, where most of your publicity will wind up. It's the news directors there that we're interested in. The talk-show contacts are entirely different people and different personalities. Those folks are the producers who determine if you get on *Oprah* or not.

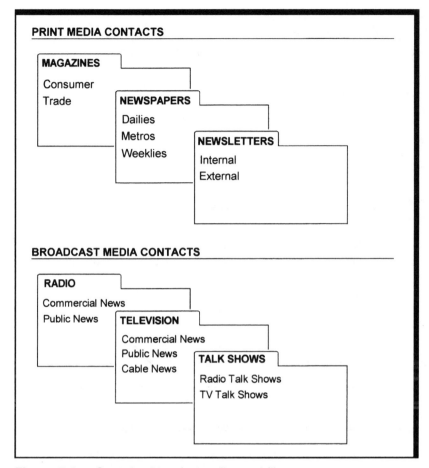

Figure 5-1. Organization of a media card file

Information You'll Need to Have

Here's the information you need for your media-contact cards, as seen in Figure 5-2. On the front of the card, be sure to include:

1. Name of publication/station/show.
2. Name of contact.
3. Street address.

LOS ANGELES TIMES   SONJA BOLLE, Editor
Times Mirror Square   Book Review Section
Los Angeles, CA 90053
(213) 237-5000

Street Address: 11771 Figueroa
               Los Angeles, CA 90005

Fax number: 213-237-4712

Deadlines: For Sunday Book Review—3 months in advance

Photo Req.:   Halftones at 85-line screen
               Negatives—right reading, emulsion-side down

Circulation: 1,411,000 Sunday
               1,127,000 Weekdays

Materials Accepted: Review kit with release, photo of cover, background information, press release. No articles. No stand-alone photos.

6/3/90—Met Sonja at NYC American Booksellers Association Conv., showed *Inventor's Marketing Handbook*. Said to send kit with book.

6/25/90—Said might send to reviewer. I pitched to time with Inventor's Convention in Pasadena. Said very possible. F/U.

7/15/90—Follow-up call. Hasn't sent yet. CB 1 month.

8/11/90—Called me a "nice nudge." Likes that I'm persistent, yet very low-key. Will send to reviewer.

9/3/90—Ran half-page review on *Inventor's Marketing Handbook*. Great coverage.

9/7/90—Sent flowers to Sonja to thank her.

Figure 5-2. Front (above) and back (below) of a sample media-contact card

4. Mailing address.
5. Telephone number.
6. Fax number.
7. Deadlines.
8. Photo requirements, if any.
9. Circulation figures or broadcast range.
10. Time of pertinent columns/broadcasts.
11. Publicity materials they accept.

On the back of the card put:

12. What was sent, when, and to whom.
13. What was aired or printed and when.

The back of the card is a tracking system that visually shows you *at a glance* how well a particular media is working. Figure 5-2 shows you how this works.

In the situation tracked in Figure 5-2, I was lucky. Timing is everything. If I hadn't asked at the *Los Angeles Times* booth at the ABA in New York; if I hadn't met Sonja; if I hadn't followed up. Oh, well, you know the rest.

Just a thought here about that "nice nudge" bit. Editors don't mind persistence as long as you're not *too* pushy about it. Yet don't forget—the key to success in publicity is three things:
FOLLOW UP——FOLLOW UP——FOLLOW UP.

Whom Should You Contact?

It's great if you have a name at a particular media. But what if you don't? Should you send it to the person by title, like "Business Editor, *Los Angeles Times*"? Absolutely not!

Editors' pet peeve number 2 is people who don't do their homework. With library access to all sorts of media directories and

Table 5-1. Media Contacts, by Job Title

MEDIA TYPE	WHOM TO CONTACT
Newspaper—metro, daily	Section editor—sports, business, lifestyle, book review, high tech, etc.
Newspaper—weekly or local	Managing editor
Magazines	Section editor; if not sure, then contact the articles editor or features editor.
Radio news	News director
Television news	Assignment editor (desk); planning desk
Radio/TV talk shows	Producers; bookers

phone calls costing very little to verify the info, there's *no excuse* for someone not having a real name.

However, perhaps you're not sure exactly whom the correct person is to call. The simple grid of Table 5-1 will explain.

Directories Galore

This is where the research discussed in Chapter 3 comes into play. There are more media directories than you can shake a stick at. Not all are good—some are just plain *horrible*. I'll tell you which ones I think are best and what they can offer you.

The media directories I especially recommend are listed in Table 5-2. (For a more complete listing of media directories, consult Appendix 7.) Most of them are available to you in the library reference room (any good county or university one, that is). Those that you will constantly use—like perhaps *Gebbie* or *Bacon's*—are worth the investment of a few hundred dollars!

You'll use several of them to develop your media-contact card file. You won't include all the names per directory—that wouldn't make sense; then you'd just buy the book—only the ones that specifically target the audiences you want to reach. Our fictional financial-planning consultant would look up *financial planning* or *money* in several of the directories, then copy onto cards the publi-

Table 5-2. Recommended Media Directories

TITLE[a]	LISTS
Bacon's Publicity Checker	Newspapers, magazines, TV, and radio (for publicists, the Bible of directories)
Broadcasting and Cable Yearbook	Electronic media: radio, TV, cable TV
Directories in Print	Thousands of directories on every conceivable subject
Directory of Women's Media	Lists of women-oriented media
Editor and Publisher International Yearbook	Daily and Sunday newspapers, foreign bureaus, clip services
Encyclopedia of Associations®	Thousands of national associations (useful for newsletter publicity, speeches)
Gale Directory of Publications and Broadcast Media	35,000 entries; also radio, TV
Gale Newsletter Directory	Corporate publications
Gebbie Press All-in-One Media Directory	Newspapers, magazines, radio, TV, syndicates, trade press (very comprehensive)
National Radio Publicity Outlets	3,500 talk shows, 4,500 local radio stations
Serials Directory	Foreign publications
Standard Periodical Directory	78,000 entries; includes foreign
TV and Cable Publicity Outlets	4,000 programs
Ulrich's International Periodicals Directory	112,000 entries; includes foreign
Working Press of the Nation	Newspapers, magazines, newsletters, radio, TV
Writer's Market	Book and magazine publishers

[a]See Appendix 7 for more complete publication information.

cation titles and related data that deal with those subjects. These would then become *possible* targets for his publicity campaign.

Certain populous cities and counties also have local media directories that can be very comprehensive and very helpful. In Los Angeles, for instance, the Publicity Club of Los Angeles puts out a complete media guide to the six-county Southern California area every year. I use it quite a bit, and it's proven to be a great resource.

The Problem with These Directories

Since 99 percent of all media directories are annuals, they are necessarily dated *the minute they're off the press.* For this reason, you MUST use several to make sure you have ALL the information you need on your contact cards.

Second reason—media personnel change jobs the way you and I turn on the water faucet—constantly. Finally, in some of the directories, the publishers themselves send the info in—so how unbiased can it be? Worse yet, many publications don't send in complete data. Again, use several directories.

Setting Up Your System

Figure 5-3 shows the simple seven-step process for setting up your card system. It should take you about a month or two, but once

STEP	ACTION
1	Pick one of the target audiences you previously determined is a high priority.
2	Go through the first directory, *Bacon's Publicity Checker*. Make a 5 × 8 card for every listing that matches the audience. (Financial = money, financial, financial management, etc.—use the index.)
3	Now, get the other directories. Fill out the cards with any missing information (see front-of-card example) from these directories.
4	Sort the cards. (See setting up card file.)
5	Make phone calls to media to confirm pertinent information: contact name, address, phone number, fax number, what they take.
6	Use the Media Analysis Grid to leverage your chances for getting story placement.
7	Now send out the 1st publicity tool, then the 2d two weeks later, then the 3d, etc.

Figure 5-3. Setting up your cards

done all you have to do is update names and addresses once a year. And that task you can pay a high school kid to do for you.

Using the Media Analysis Grid

We use this to determine exactly which publicity tools (see next chapter) to send out and in what order. We know, for example, that almost every media takes a news release, which is why it's so important to learn how to write them. But what about the other publicity tools of the trade? When should we send a stand-alone photo? Or do an article? The key is to leverage your time and your resources. If only 2 out of 12 targeted publications take a full article, it's silly to spend time writing that first. Do it last, and give yourself *enough time* to do it right!

Table 5-3 is a sample grid, all filled in for our computer-consultant friends. We'll set up a situation involving the *Los Angeles Times*

Table 5-3. Media Analysis Grid—Daily Newspapers

PUBLICITY TOOL	WILL NEWSPAPER ACCEPT?			
	LAT	NYT	OCR	WSJ
Standard press release	Yes	Yes	Yes	Yes
Photo with press release	Yes	Yes	Yes	Yes
Stand-alone photo	Yes	Yes	Yes	
Letter to the editor	Yes	Yes	Yes	Yes
Feature article (freelance copy)				
Op-ed piece (opinion)	Yes	Yes	Yes	Yes
Media advisory (for an event)	Yes		Yes	
New product or service release	Yes		Yes	Yes
Calendar listing—business section	Yes	Yes	Yes	
Personnel listing (movers and shakers)	Yes	Yes	Yes	Yes
Press kit (includes release, backgrounder, fact sheet, photo)	SIA	SIA	SIA	SIA

Key. LAT: *Los Angeles Times;* NYT: *New York Times;* OCR: *Orange County Register;* SIA: Send if asked (send only after sending standard release, when contact person asks for it, not before); WSJ: *The Wall Street Journal.*

(LAT), *Orange County Register* (OCR), *New York Times* (NYT), and *The Wall Street Journal* (WSJ). Remember, the grid is filled in from your contact cards.

THE NEWS RELEASE

The news release is the backbone of your publicity campaign—it's the most important tool you'll use. From it you'll be able to create featurette articles (under 750 words), full feature articles, and other important publicity tools. If you master how to write it, where to send it, and who to send it to, you should get more than 50 percent of your releases placed. There are two basic rules to help you write your news release: the five *W*s and *H* formula and the inverted pyramid style of writing.

Five Ws and H Formula

This is the standard formula we all learned in high school English—who, what, where, when, why, and how. These are standard questions that each release must answer, and answer completely, or get tossed in the garbage by an overworked editor. Some of the questions you should make sure to answer in your release are:

Who are you, your company, and/or your client?
What specifically is your service, or the story about?
Where is your service available? Or **where** is your event being held?
When is it available? **When** is an event being held?
Why is your consultancy unique? **Why** is it different?
How does it work?

The order you put them in determines how strong the release, hence your presence in the paper, will be. We call the rule for ordering the *inverted pyramid formula*—taking the most important point first, the next-most-important second, and so on.

Let's take our financial-planning consultants as an example. Suppose they've decided to offer a free retirement seminar (a publicity method) to Chamber of Commerce members. They'll use a standard release (main method 1) to get the word out. We'll do the writing for them for now. Let's lead with the who (the consultants), since that's what they want to emphasize first—the who. (What you emphasize first is called the *lead*.)

> John Jones, CFP, Senior Partner of Jones and Smith [WHO] will present a seminar "Retire before You're 50" [WHAT] at the Chino Chamber of Commerce, 14144 Central Ave. [WHERE], on Monday, September 14, 1998, 7:00 P.M. [WHEN] Attendees will learn six essential steps to making themselves debt-free [HOW] within one year. Jones stated that chamber members can learn previously unknown planning methods to enjoy their golden years while they can. [WHY]

This is a typical starting point for a release. It follows the conventional pattern in order. Begin learning with this type, a who lead, then adapt to stronger leads. Reason to adapt? A who lead, when you're an unknown, will normally give you a calendar listing and not much more.

Now, suppose we wanted to emphasize the reason for the seminar first—a stronger lead.

Figure 5-4 blocks it out. When we turn this into prose, here's how the first two graphs might look:

> "Most Chinoites have had it. They want to retire while they still can afford to enjoy their golden years. [WHY] And they can't!" says John Jones, CFP, Senior Partner of Jones and Smith, financial planning consultants. [WHO]

WHY

Golden years; retire before 50

WHO

John Jones, CFP, Jones and Smith

WHAT

Seminar, "Retire before You're 50"

HOW

Six essential steps

WHERE

Chino Chamber of Commerce

WHEN

Monday, September 14, 1998

Figure 5-4. Press release blocking tool with a why lead

Jones has an answer. His free "Retire before You're 50" seminar [WHAT], which teaches the six essential steps necessary to make this happen [HOW], will be held at the Chamber of Commerce office, 14144 Central Ave., Chino, [WHERE] on Monday, September 14, 1998, from 7:00 to 9:00 P.M. [WHEN]

OK, it's your turn. Use Figure 5-5 to list the five Ws and H for your first story, then prioritize according to the inverted pyramid formula.

News-Release Holes

One of the surest ways to kill a release is to forget some vital information. Sure, you've put your name as a contact person at the top, and you've included your phone number. But don't expect the

CATEGORY	INFORMATION	RANK
WHO		
WHAT		
WHERE		
WHEN		
WHY		
HOW		

Figure 5-5. Ranking your five *W*s and *H*

media to call you back if something's missing—like a phone number, date of event, or time. *They* simply do not have the time. They'll just junk your release in the round file.

What's a *hole?* If the above release had stated "September 14, 1998, at 7 o'clock," THAT WOULD BE A HUGE HOLE! Is it 7 A.M. or 7 P.M.? And don't forget addresses. That's why I put in the exact address of the Chino Chamber. *Never assume* that the readers, or the editor, knows where a specific place is. If they do, they'll delete. Don't *you* delete it. After all, what if they run your release verbatim? It has happened, you know.

More Rules for Releases

When I edited my newspaper in San Diego, I got tons of releases in every imaginable format. Only one format is right. Figure 5-6 shows a sample news release with all the elements filled in.

REECE FRANKLIN & ASSOCIATES
14911 Rolling Ridge Drive
Chino Hills, CA 91709

(714) 393-8525

FOR IMMEDIATE RELEASE

For Further Information:
Reece Franklin (714) 393-8525

SMALL BUSINESS LECTURE SERIES SET FOR MAMMOTH LAKES

(Mammoth Lakes, CA) - (October 1, 1988) - A series of three small business workshops has been set for Mammoth Lakes October 23 - 25, to be held at the Parks and Recreation Office at 6 p.m. The subjects include "How To Market Your Small Business, How To Get FREE Publicity, and How To Advertise and Promote Your Small Business."

The series is being conducted by Reece Franklin, founder of the Small Business Assistance Center of Chino Hills, California. Mr. Franklin conducts numerous seminars/workshops for small business around the Southern California area, and was approached by the Town Council to bring his expertise and knowledge to the merchants here.

"There is a big difference between marketing in Los Angeles and marketing in Mammoth Lakes," said Franklin. "While the tactics are basically the same anywhere, we will focus on which ones will work best for these economic conditions, and how to apply them to this specific situation."

For further information, contact Mary Cahill at the Parks and Recreation Department at 619-555-7777.

###

MARKETING □ ADVERTISING □ PUBLIC RELATIONS

Figure 5-6. Author's press release for seminar event

Look closely at how it's set up. Here are some tips on how it's done.

1. Use Letterhead. Put the release on letterhead. But don't have extra letterhead typeset with the words *news release* on it.

Journalists aren't dumb, folks. They know it's a release when they see it, since you put it in correct format.

2. Be Brief.   Keep the release to one page, two at the most. If you have more to say, create a backgrounder or fact sheet (show you how in the next chapter). One of *my* pet peeves as an editor of a computer newspaper was public relations firms and companies that sent in releases with page after page of redundant, pedantic, B-O-R-I-N-G prose. Some even as long as 16 pages! Like I really had the time to understand their technobabble! Puh-leeze!

3. Double-Space.   Double-space the release to leave enough room for editing or comments on the page. And give them enough margin room on the side, at least one inch.

4. Make It Easy to Reach You.   Put the contact name (your) and number at the top. Editors just may want to call you for more info or to flesh out (newspaper term) the story. They can't if they can't reach you.

5. Be Pithy.   Only four or five short graphs per release, please. If they want more, they'll ask. Keep your sentences short—about 15 words max per sentence. And no more than two sentences per graph. What does this mean? Keep your writing tight, brief, to-the-point. Don't waste words; *every* one counts.

6. Use a brief, powerful headline.   In your headline, tell what the story is about in a short, simple sentence or two. Make it positive, and show the benefit the readers will get. If you can't do that, you don't have a handle on what you want to say. Rewrite, baby!

7. Keep It Simple.   Write in simple eighth-grade-level style. That's a 14-year-old, folks. No fancy $500 words. Not *utilize*, but *use*; not *consultation*, but *he consulted*. Keep it simple. (A good grammar checker that also calculates reading level is Grammatik VI. Get it. It's only $99.)

8. Tell Them When It's Over

Use "-end-" or "###" as a last line to show the end. Editors are not mind readers. They're pretty smart, but sometimes they're not sure where the end of your release is. So tell 'em. And if they give your release to a staff member and say "run verbatim," they *have* to know where it ends.

Notice how I structured the release in Figure 5-6. I knew it would probably get a calendar listing or perhaps an inch or two. That's why I started with the what rather than the who. Also, I knew that the Mammoth Lakes business community didn't know who I was but *did* know who the town council (the sponsor) was. That's why I'm in the second graph. Downplay your ego and you'll get more results.

WHAT SHOULD YOU SEND?

Most consultants, and small-business people in general, want to load up the editor and/or reporter with paper, thinking it's the one chance they have to "get the info to them." WRONG, WRONG, WRONG! Just send a simple release along with an action photo. Nothing else. Cover letter? Why? To tell them there's a release in the envelope? Waste of time and money.

Most people when using a cover letter end it with "We'd appreciate any coverage you can give us." Of course they would. But saying it won't make it so. Save your breath, folks. No cover letter with a release, OK? Table 5-4 shows what to send.

Photo

What do I mean by *action photo?* Not the standard you-shaking-hands-with-your-client. That's boring. Or the firing-squad shot—you standing in a group of three to five people, ramrod straight, and all of you looking like you're about to be executed. Or worse,

Table 5-4. What to Send with Your News Release, by Media

MEDIA	WHAT DO YOU SEND?
Print	News release, action photo, fact sheet (optional)
Radio News	News release (audio optional), fact sheet (optional)
TV News	News release and slide or video news release
Talk Shows	News release, video showing how you interview

the mug shot of you grinning ear to ear. My advice—don't mug and cease firing! Instead, use a photo showing live action of you consulting with a client, with their product or service in action. The caption will explain what it is you're doing—making their business better.

Audiotape

An *audio news release* is basically you-as-announcer discussing your story. Don't read your printed release verbatim. It's boring. But *do* show emotion, and modulate your voice. You want to help the news director understand what a great guest or news source you'll be. (Some people sound just awful on the air. If this is you, just send the written release.) Use your cassette recorder. Nothing fancy. Ten minutes should do it.

Videotape

A *video news release* (VNR) is another story entirely. This is an actual two-minute segment, *professionally done,* that highlights you consulting with a client or two. Base the story on some real-world struggle (the human-interest factor, remember?) and how you solved it.

To do a VNR correctly, I suggest you contact a professional video company that specializes in them. They'll script it, tape it, edit it, then send it to a list of over 100 TV stations via satellite feed. The cost? Around $3,000. Whoa! You couldn't do it as well yourself for half again or double the cost, believe me.

Just an aside—60 percent or more of the "major" stories on the nightly network news are VNRs from companies. In other words, planted stories. The public never knows this. Take a look next time when you see a story that seems to be highly positive about a particular company and the problems it's solving. Chances are it's a VNR.

Slides

If you can't do a VNR, *slides* are very useful for TV news. Remember, TV is a visual medium. So if you only send a written release, you're shooting yourself in the foot. Send a color slide. It's more likely to be used.

Interview tape

You send an interview tape to the producers of talk shows—we'll get into this more in a later chapter. For now, just understand the reason for sending a video of you in a "mock" interview: They can't see how you're going to "perform" in a written release. They need to know you can be lively, entertaining, and so on.

Don't spend a lot of money on this. A simple camcorder recording will do (use a tripod, of course). Practice until you have the answers to several *preset* questions down cold. You'll look like a pro.

THE PRESS KIT

Most consultants get very excited about putting together a so-called press kit. In fact, many consulting books suggest that's the first thing you do. I don't! You only send a press kit when the media asks you for one. So why spend thousands of dollars on fancy covers, stationery, and inserts when they'll burn a hole in your pocket—and take up space in your garage.

Yes, you should know what goes in a kit. But you can put one together in about two weeks, so there's no need to jump the gun.

Basic Press Kit

Here's what I recommend for the consultant's press kit (the figures are examples drawn from my own press kit):

1. **The news release**—this one about you and your latest project. Update every six months, or redo based on the current project (see Figure 5-7).
2. **Fact sheet**—a simple, one-sided one-page who, what, where, when, why, and how sheet that tells the media, at a quick glance, exactly what's going on (see Figure 5-8).
3. **Personal bio**—a résumé redone in press form (see Figure 5-9).
4. **Action photo**—again, you with your happy-camper client.
5. **Print clip sheet** (for print media)—articles by and about you, cut out and pasted onto one legal-sized (8.5 × 14 inch) sheet, single sided (see Figures 5-10 and 5-11).
6. **Electronic contact sheet** (for broadcast media)—simply a listing of radio or TV news and/or talk shows you've been on (see Figure 5-12).
7. **Binder or cover**—plain, glossy white. No fancy letter-foil, thermoplate, or four-color process. Use a simple label on the front, with your name, address, and phone number. Put the label in the lower right-hand corner.

AAJA PUBLISHING COMPANY
P. O. Box 2667
Chino, CA 91708-2667

For   Immediate   Release

For   Further   Information:
Nadine   Johnson,   714-393-8525

AMERICA STILL STRONG FOR INVENTORS, SAYS AUTHOR

(Los Angeles) - Disputing the naysayers who claim that America has fallen behind in technology and invention, Reece Franklin, author of the new INVENTOR'S MARKETING HANDBOOK: A COMPLETE GUIDE TO SELLING AND PROMOTING YOUR INVENTION, (AAJA Publishing, ISBN 0-9623938-7-8, $19.95), has something to say about that.

"Every couple of years, the doom and gloom merchants bark their same old weary song," said Franklin. "But the truth is, American has never been better. Look at all the computer technology coming from the United States. Look at the recent success of Voyager II. That happened because somebody dreamed about it, and invented processes to make things happen!" he continued.

Because he feels so strongly about American inventors, Franklin wrote the book to help them promote their inventions even more. The book includes chapters on selling, advertising, promotion, publicity, and trade shows—all vital marketing tools the inventor may need at some time in his career.

Written in simple, easy-to-read style, the book is available for $19.95 plus $2 shipping/handling from AAJA Publishing Company, P.O. Box 2667, Chino, CA 91708.

# # #

Figure 5-7.   Basic press release, from author's files

FACT SHEET

WHO: **REECE FRANKLIN AND ASSOCIATES**, A Full Service Marketing/Advertising firm.

WHAT: Announces new Institute for Small Business

WHERE: 12755 Foothill Blvd., Claremont, CA 91794

WHEN: GRAND OPENING, FRIDAY, NOVEMBER 10, 1995, 6 P.M. TO 9 P.M.

WHY: "There is no concentrated, quick study program in sequence for small business to learn the skills they need for securing loans, marketing, or promoting their business. This school will teach them, in 10-week sequential classes, everything they need to know."

HOW: Small business will benefit by learning real-world, hands-on techniques they can use immediately to help them grow.

Figure 5-8.   Sample fact sheet for basic press kit from author's files

---

BIOGRAPHY

Reece Franklin is currently president of MarketSmarts, a Chino-based consulting firm, specializing in marketing, advertising, and public relations for small and medium sized businesses.

He gives over 100 seminars and speeches per year in southern California to industry and trade groups, as well as small business.

He was founding Chairman of the Chaffey College Small Business Task Force and is currently chairman of the Chino Valley Chamber Small Business Committee. He is secretary of the Inland Empire Chapter of the American Marketing Association.

Mr. Franklin is also a member of the Professional Communicators of Southern California, and the Book Publicists of Southern California.

Reece has been called the guru of Inland Empire Marketing by the Inland Daily Bulletin, and has been featured in Inc. Magazine, Entrepreneur, Los Angeles Times, Orange County Register, and dozens of other national publications.

He is the author of <u>Inventor's Marketing Handbook,</u> <u>How to Sell and Promote Your Idea, Project, or Invention</u>, and <u>How to Market Your Home Based Business</u>. His new book, <u>Consultant's Guide To Publicity</u>, will be published in April by John Wiley and Sons.

Figure 5-9.   Sample consultant bio, from author's press kit

National Inventor's Day Promotion

Staff Photo by Nancy Newnew
Author of the Inventor's Marketing Handbook, Reece Franklin of Chino, wrote a letter to President Bush, encouraging him to give the Feb. 11 Inventors Day national recognition.

Holiday suggested to honor inventors

By William Diepenbrock
Staff Writer

The Northern Star Monday February 12, 1990

Alumnus lobbies for national day

by Alyce Malchiodi

(Star-Progress photo by Jack Hancock)
AUTHOR, AUTHOR! — Reece Franklin, formerly of La Habra, is bringing his new book to local audiences Feb. 17, when he conducts an Inventors' Marketing Workshop of Cal State Fullerton. Participants in the all-day seminar will receive a copy of the book, "Inventor's Marketing Handbook."

Former La Habran going to bat for nation's inventors

By Anne Davidson
DBP Staff Writer

Lecturer launches effort to declare day for inventors

By CHRISTOPHER KRUEGER
California staff writer

Reece Franklin
...university lecturer

Bakersfield Californian 2/11/60

SELL IT — Reece Franklin, a Chino Hills resident, shows the Inventors Marketing Handbook he authored which he uses as a text in his seminars on marketing inventions. Mr.

Chino Hills man lobbies for 'Inventor's Day'

By Marianne Napoles
Staff Writer

OCC teacher wants to honor inventors

By DEBORA SAKAMOTO
Daily Pilot correspondent

Reece Franklin

Figure 5-10. Multiple clip sheet from author's press kit

76

Noteworthy Advice

Even marketing experts need good marketing plans, and Reece Franklin is no exception. How about taking his idea of using a seminar to find out more about your prospective clients? The students walk away with new information . . . and you come away with client profiles!

Franklin says the key is using students' business cards to create a personalized mailing list. By jotting down the class his students attended, the date, and the problems they mentioned in class, he can write each student a personal letter explaining how his consulting service could help solve their difficulty. The result? Instant marketing tailored to the individual—without having to meet with or talk to every student. "Everyone's needs are so different," says Franklin. "You can't generate their interest in any other way."

Figure 5-11. Clip sheet with single story to promote author's consultancy. *Reprinted with permission from* Entrepreneur Magazine *June 1992.*

Radio and TV Show Appearances by Reece Franklin		
Television	"Success Forum"	"Morning Show"
"Sun Up San Diego"	KCOX	KFND
KFMB	San Diego, CA	Fargo, ND
San Diego, CA	*Radio*	"Midnight With Art"
Evening News	"Milk and Honey"	KVEG AM
KERO	KELC AM	Las Vegas
Bakersfield, CA	San Diego, CA	Noon News
"News at Nine"	"Money Talks"	WTOP
KCAL	KIEV	Washington, DC
Los Angeles, CA	Glendale, CA	"Sunday Scene"
"Inventor's Forum"	Noon News	WLS
KCOX	KOA	Chicago, IL
San Diego, CA	Denver, CO	

Figure 5-12. Sample electronic contact sheet

Expanded Press Kit

Once in a while it might be good to add a few things to your press kit, especially if you're dealing with a lot of national media, like *The Wall Street Journal* or *Los Angeles Times*. To the basic kit just discussed I'd add an opinion piece on a controversial topic that highlights you as an expert and a practice brochure (a good one that shows why you're an expert and what you do. But no puff; just facts). Finally, one or two full articles on you, reproduced on your letterhead, and a case history or two (past client winners). And that's it.

Speaker's Press Kit

If you intend to use speaking as a publicity tool, which you should, there's a very distinct difference between a speaker's press kit and a regular press kit. Before you get to this stage in your publicity, I suggest you buy Dottie Walter's book *Speak and Grow Rich* (Englewood Cliffs, N.J.: Prentice-Hall, 1989). Here's what Dottie recommends (again, the figures are examples drawn from press kits for my clients and myself):

- Your brochure or one-sheet (see Figure 5-13).
- Your topic title and speech outline.
- Video demo tape of a live presentation.
- Audio demo tape of a live presentation.
- Copies of testimonial letters (see Figures 5-14 and 5-15).
- Lists of clients for whom you have spoken.
- Reprints of articles you've written on this topic (see Figure 5-16).
- A menu of services you offer (see Figure 5-17).
- Your fee schedule (see Figure 5-18).
- Newspaper and magazine story reprints about you and your work, written by others (see Figure 5-19).
- Bio (see Figure 5-20).

MARIE HAYASHI REICHELT

"Human Resources Development"

Marie Hayashi Reichelt is a successful professional with a background in human resources, multicultural diversity and career development. She brings many talents to perform over 100 platform presentations each year. She assists her clients in developing organizational culture, assisting participants in creating work environments that promote diversity and value diversity. She was born in Japan, and English is her second language.

Marie will share her techniques and lifelong skills with her upbeat personality and humor. You will learn real-world applications that can be used immediately.

Some of the organizations that have been clients are:

• Mattel Toys	• Loma Linda University Medical Center
• Adohr Farms	• Fairchilds
• Mt. San Antonio College	• Cal Poly Pomona
• TRW Technar	• Bird Medical Products

Affiliations:

American Society for Training and Development (ASTD), The Association of Human Resources Professionals (PIRA), Toastmasters International, Japan-American Society.

Topics:

• **Yes, There Is Life After Aerospace** — Learn lifelong skills to achieve full career potential.

• **Preventing Sexual Harassment** — Decrease your sexual harassment liabilities by learning how to recognize and control them at the root.

• **Affirmative Action and EEO — How to Avoid the Courts** — Minimize AA/EEO litigation by learning how to interview, motivate and discipline employees the *right* way.

• **Sugarcoating Diversity** — Learn the meaning of Sexism, Racism, Classism and Ageism, and work and live more harmoniously with each other.

• **The Rising Sun — The Real Story of Working with Japan** — Learn to minimize faux pas in working with the Japanese —absorb some of its culture and language.

• **Walking the Tightrope (Leadership Skills for Women)** — Become all that you can be — empower yourself to be the next leader.

Keynotes • Workshops • Custom Programs • In-house Training

APB Associates

758 N. Quince Avenue • Upland, CA 91786 • (909) 982-7595

Figure 5-13. One-sheet, from speaker's press kit

- Black-and-white (B/W), glossy photos of you posed and in action before an audience.
- Cover letter to potential buyer of speaking services.
- Contract copy (not for the media—clients only).

Corporate Office:
9050 Friars Rd.
Suite 400
San Diego, CA 92108
(619) 563-4800
FAX (619) 563-9850

POSTALANNEX⁺
Your Home Office .

April 24, 1994

Mr. Reece Franklin
14911 Rolling Ridge Drive
Chino Hills, CA
91709

Dear Reece,

Thank you for your excellent presentation on "Creating Effective Ads" at the PostalAnnex+ National Convention. Our franchisees were very impressed with the information they gathered from your presentation. I have only heard positive comments.

I am confident that they will be implementing many of the good ideas that you shared with them. I know our franchisees will be using their advertising dollars more effectively in their future advertising campaigns as a result of your informative seminar.

I hope that we will have the opportunity to work with you again in the future. Reece, thank you again for a great seminar!

Sincerely,

David Wilkey
Director of Marketing

Figure 5-14. Sample testimonial letter, from speaker's press kit

"It's Your Business"
1994 Small Business Conference

April 14, 1994

Mr. Reece Franklin
14911 Rolling Ridge Drive
Chino Hills, CA 91709

Dear Reece:

Thank you for giving of your time and talents to be a speaker for the *It's Your Business* 1994 Small Business Conference. Your seminar, "The 3 Keys to Marketing Success," was an excellent addition to the program. We promised the small business owners a conference full of presentations that dealt with the basics, and due to the expertise of speakers like you, we believe we were successful at meeting their needs.

The evaluations that were turned in by conference attendees indicated that they were very pleased with the quality of the speakers and presentations, as well as with the overall conference.

Again, thank you for helping us to make March 15 a memorable day for the small business community. Your contribution as a speaker is greatly appreciated. We look forward to having another conference in 1995 and will certainly consider having you as a speaker at that time.

Sincerely,

Linda Pinson
Conference Chair

LP:ocs

NAWBO Administrative Office
17621 Irvine Blvd., Suite 204, Tustin, CA 92680
Tel: (714) 730-6100   FAX: (714) 730-5016

Figure 5-15.   Sample testimonial letter, from speaker's press kit

TOOLS OF THE TRADE

C O L U M N

MARKETING

Choosing a
Public Relations Agency

REECE A. FRANKLIN

Y ou've decided to enhance your business image by starting a public relations campaign. The work involved seems staggering, so you decide to hire an agency or publicist.

Where do you look, and what do you look for? Do you choose an agency out of the yellow pages, or call the nearest chapter of Publicists Anonymous?

The answer is, of course, neither. There are some very firm and sensible rules a business should follow in hiring a public relations firm. Here are the basics:

1. Understand what you want. Do you want public relations or publicity? There is a difference. Public relations is the umbrella encompassing a complete campaign, which might include speech writing, media relations, policy statements, preparing for journalists' questions, article preparation, and other collateral materials.

Publicity is one part of the entire picture, or the gasoline for the engine. It is the day-to-day phone calls, writing, and placing of your story to the media.

When you understand what you want, whether it is public relations or just publicity, you'll know whom you need to call for help.

2. Free-lancers vs. full-service agencies. Free-lance publicists accept jobs on an hourly or project basis. You may assign them separate tasks, such as writing a news release, or an entire project.

A full-service agency, on the other hand, does what its name implies: offers you all the services at its disposal, from press releases to campaign strategy and tactics.

3. Understand what outside services can do. An outside service can provide you with help that you cannot provide for yourself. Some basic considerations:

- They can augment weak areas in your staff.
- They can offer expertise where you have no proven track record.
- They can be objective and provide fresh, impartial ideas.
- They identify your problems and weaknesses.
- They can act as catalysts to initiate change.
- They can instruct your staff on how to follow-up for future campaigns.
- They can use their contact base to gain influence for you.

All of these should be part of the package of expertise an agency brings to you when offering their services.

4. Use referrals to get the names of reliable agencies. The first step in choosing an agency is to get referrals from other businesses that have used p.r. firms. If you cannot get at least six names, call the Inland Empire Chapter of the Public Relations Society of America (PRSA). They have a referral hotline which can match your needs with the proper type of agency.

5. Make sure the pro is a pro. While membership in societies is not a guarantee of competence, a professional firm which is a member of the PRSA is less likely to cause you problems.

6. Don't get caught in the specialty trap. Although many firms specialize in certain types of businesses, it is my experience that the agency with a varied background,can be more beneficial.

7. Do not be misled by any guarantee, written or otherwise. The publicist or agency who guarantees you space in a publication, or a spot on *The Tonite Show*, is not worth having. No respectable firm ever promises you coverage.

8. Make sure you feel comfortable with the agency. If you feel the slightest bit uneasy about going into a relationship with an agency, then keep on looking. Your relationship with the p.r. firm must be founded on mutual trust, respect, and comfort in working together.

9. Work with your agency. My philosophy is that my clients know their business better than I do, and I know public relations better then they do.

When you hire someone for their advice, and they give it, take it. Sure, you'll disagree. But if your agency says, "In our professional opinion, if you follow course A, you're making a mistake," then heed their warning! •

Reece Franklin *owns a public relations agency in Chino Hills and teaches public relations at Chaffey College Community Education.*

Figure 5-16. Sample article reprint, from speaker's press kit

PROGRAM FEES AND EXPENSES

SINGLE PROGRAM FEES

Half Day—30 minutes to 3 hours: $1250
Full Day—up to 6 hours: $2100
Panel Participant: $500
Pre-consulting (per hour) $250
Customized program (per hour) $300
Local program (within So. Cal.) .... deduct 25%

MULTIPLE PROGRAMS

Additional programs at same event

1. Between 2 and 5 programs—$300 fee reduction per program
2. Between 6 and 10 programs—$600 fee reduction per program
3. Eleven or more program—$1,050 fee reduction per program

DEPOSITS AND CANCELLATION POLICY

The deposit is 50% of agreed fee, and is required upon confirmation of the booking. In the event of program cancellation, Reece Franklin & Associates will re-book on a mutually convenient date. If program is cancelled by client and not rescheduled, deposit constitutes full and complete settlement.

TRAVEL EXPENSES

All fees are as quoted, plus travel expenses. Full coach airfare will be booked by Reece Franklin & Associates. Travel and expenses will be invoiced after the program has been completed.

ACCOMMODATIONS

Speaker's accommodations should be direct billed to your organization.

SUPPORT MATERIALS.

Materials for participants will be invoiced as quoted.

AUDIO AND VIDEO RECORDING

Any non-profit distribution of the program within your organization is permitted, given a master copy of such recording is supplied to and approved by the speaker.

BOOKS AND TAPES

Educational support materials can be made available.

Figure 5-17. Sample menu of speaking services, from author's press kit.

FEE SCHEDULE

Full-page ad (7 × 10 inch)	$500
Annual report	$5000
Feature article	$750
Booklet	$800
Brochure (Slim Jim)	$100 per panel
Brochure (7 × 10 inch)	$200 per page
Business plan (no research)	$2000
(with research)	$4000–$6000
Case history	$1000
Direct-mail package (leads)	$1500
Direct-mail package (M.O.)	$3000
Editorial services	$65–$85 per hour
Film, slide presentation, or other audio-visual script	$100 per minute
Instruction manual	$65 per page
Newsletter	$250 per page
Press release	$300
Proposal	$55 per hour
Radio commercial	$300
Sales letter	$750–$1250
Speech, 20-minute	$2500
TV commercial	$1000
Day rates (per diem) for freelance writing services	$750
Hourly rate for research	$95
Consulting	$125 per hour

Figure 5-18. Sample fee schedule, from speaker's press kit (author's)

The Orange County Register

Business

Saturday, July 25, 1992

INVENTIVE MARKETING

A good creation is only the start; the real success is when it sells

What's the good of inventing a better mousetrap if nobody knows about it?

That's exactly the problem with thousands of terrific inventions. Even if they make it beyond the pepperoni-pizza-and-root-beer dreams of their creators into actual prototypes, they're still a long way from Kmart's shelves.

It's Your Business hates to see great ideas go to waste. So Problem 197 addresses this very issue of how an inventor should market an idea to make it successful and not just another deposit in the landfill of might-have-beens.

Mike Peng of Huntington Beach is determined to be in the former category.

After Peng's father suffered a stroke, keeping track of the medication schedule and quantities was a problem. The teenager was working two jobs to support the family, so he needed to leave his father instructions on how many pills to take and when.

Peng put the prescribed dose in a plastic bag and attached a Post-It note with instructions. Hey, he figured, this self-stick note and pouch had all kinds of uses. A collector could insert a baseball card and label it. A programmer could put in computer disks with instructions. A diligent mom could pack a snack with message attached.

Peng calls his invention Post-Script Plus. He's already started limited production and marketing while the patent is pending and he works out mass-production methods.

"I sent samples to 30 major publishers, and already Fortune magazine's product-watch column has contacted me," Peng said.

Next he plans to display his product at inventors shows. And if he's not selling hundreds of thousands of PostScript Pluses after that, "I would put an ad in The Wall Street Journal."

Not a bad start.

But for long-term success the inventor needs a comprehensive approach to marketing, says Reece Franklin, author of "Inventor's Marketing Handbook," a complete guide to selling and promoting an invention.

"Most inventors are not salespeople, they're technicians," Franklin said. "They're good at what they do but not good at telling the world."

That's why just 1 percent of all ideas patented ever reach the marketplace, he says.

How can inventors increase those odds?

"The first thing is to ask if the invention is sellable in terms of

JAN NORMAN

It's Your Business

packaging, appearance, price," Franklin said.

An inventor must consider whether a product is too big to fit on a store shelf and whether it costs $1,793.27 to manufacture but customers say they would pay only $12 for such an item.

Next, Franklin says, is determining who needs or wants your product. "Inventors always say 'everyone in the world.' If you sell to everyone you won't sell anything to anyone. Pick a niche and fill it."

Franklin, who teaches marketing classes and workshops for inventors, has a student who sells earthquake-survival kits. He's ringing up healthy sales by targeting the employee stores at major corporations.

Franklin will teach invention-marketing fundamentals at the International Inventors and Entrepreneurs Expo from July 30 to Aug. 2 at the Queen Mary in Long Beach. His book is available at the expo or by mail from AAJA Publishing, 14911 Rolling Ridge Drive, Chino Hills 91709.

"Marketing and salesmanship are always where inventors fail," said Alan Tratner, the expo's promoter and president of Inventors Workshop International in Camarillo. "That's why we have 75 workshops at the show to teach inventors how to do such things as distribute their inventions, sell, use infomercials and mail order."

Before marketing, Franklin says, the inventor also needs to be brutally honest about the competition. One inventor said he had no competitors, but Franklin found 157 by going to one trade show for that industry.

Every product has three categories of potential competitors, Franklin says. Direct competitors are selling the same product. Indirect competitors sell products that are similar in consumers' minds. And third are dissimilar products that compete for attention and limited consumer dollars.

For example, a winery competes directly with every other wine in the cellar. It competes

Please see IYB/2

An inventor can save time, money and a lot of anxiety by spending a few days in the public library. Franklin says. Before spending thousands of dollars applying for patents or making prototypes, thumb through such tomes as the Thomas Register of American Manufacturers, a 21-volume compilation of manufacturers and their products. Maybe the product already exists somewhere.

Other books can help the inventor identify likely customers. Most reference librarians are delighted to point you to the right sources.

If this search encourages you to proceed with your idea, you need to identify its uniqueness, Franklin says. "Don't knock the competition; say why your invention is better."

The student with the earthquake-preparedness kits made sure they contained every item recommended by the American Red Cross. He could honestly put on the label that the product meets Red Cross standards.

Then he packaged the kits in plastic buckets, which made them more crush-resistant and distinctive from dozens of other earthquake-preparedness products on the shelf.

Next make up a few prototypes and show them to potential buyers, Franklin says. Sounds easy, but it's the toughest step for inventors, who usually think everyone is out to steal their ideas.

But at this point you're miles ahead of any thief, so ask around before you spend $10,000 on production.

And don't just ask your mom and your drinking buddies.

"Talk to 250 people and store buyers," Franklin said. "Would they buy it, and how much would they be willing to pay? If you won't show it to anyone until you're ready to sell, then it won't sell."

Swap meets are great places to test-market an invention, says Donald BonAsia, inventor of Forkchops, which combine chopsticks with knives and forks. He sold thousands of Forkchops at the Orange County Marketplace at the county fairgrounds in Costa Mesa.

That experience gave BonAsia confidence to send news releases about Forkchops to food sections of major newspapers nationwide. Many have mentioned the product. And that coverage has brought him

Figure 5-19. Single clip sheet from author's press kit—shared story. *Reprinted with permission of* The Orange County Register, *copyright 1992.*

REECE FRANKLIN

Reece Franklin has been called the "guru" of marketing of the Inland Empire by the Inland Valley Daily Bulletin, a Southern California regional newspaper. He is recognized as an innovator in teaching Common Sense Marketing to over 3,000 small and medium size businesses in California since 1988.

His audiences range from business conferences to associations and trade organizations, from 25 to 250 participants at a time. Some of Mr. Franklin's clients include National Employees Service and Recreation Association, Dale Carnegie Franchisees, American Institute of Architects, California Auto Body Association, California School Employees Association, Association of Better Computer Dealers, American Society for Training & Development, and the California Association of Enrolled Agents.

His topics include Common Sense Marketing, Power Up Your Business, High Power Publicity, Powerful Promo Materials, Advertising That Sells, and Turn on Your Dream Machine.

Reece began his career as a professional fund raiser in 1973, and moved into promotions and media in 1977. Before establishing his company in 1988, Mr. Franklin was Regional Sales Director for BAM Publications, GMW Communications, and the IT Media Group. He was Associate Publisher with Singman Publications, a regional specialty newspaper group.

He has been featured in Inc. Magazine, Entrepreneur, Los Angeles Times, Orange County Register, and dozens of other business and regional publications. His radio appearances include both regional and national business shows, and was a regular "invention" segment host on Sun Up San Diego. He is the author of Inventor's Marketing Handbook, How to Sell and Promote Your Idea, Project, or Invention, and How to Market Your Home Based Business.

Reece is a member of the American Marketing Association, Professional Communicators Association, and Association of Professional Consultants.

In 1992, Reece started his current company, MarketSmarts, a results oriented marketing firm that uses common sense approaches to the difficult problems of today's marketplace.

Reece was educated at Northern Illinois University, and holds a Bachelor's degree in International Relations. He is married, and has five grandchildren.

Figure 5-20. Sample speaker's bio, from author's kit

Special Book-Review Press Kit

If you're a consultant who's written at least one book (and you should—it makes you an "instant" expert), there's a special type of press kit you need to generate coverage and book reviews. Since it's beyond the scope of this book to cover book review publicity in depth, let me recommend you read two of the best— Dan Poynter's *Self-Publishing Manual,* 8th edition (Santa Barbara, CA: Para, 1995) and Barbara Gaughn's (pronounced "gone") *Book Blitz: Getting Your Book in the News* (Best-Seller Books, 1994). They're masters, and they've already written the best on the subject.

Barbara, Dan, and Peggy Glenn, my three gurus of book publicity, recommend the following for your book-review press kit (Figures 5-19 through 5-23 provide you with samples):

- Book brochure or flyer (see Figure 5-21).
- News release (see Figure 5-22).
- Your photo (see Figure 5-23).
- Photo or reprint of book cover (if completed).
- Your biography (see Figure 5-24).
- Articles written about you or about other books you've written (see Figure 5-25).
- Author available for interviews (see Figure 5-26).
- Reviewer's fact sheet (see Figure 5-27).
- Extra covers of your book (to be used as folders).
- Sample Q-and-A (for electronic interviewers), if any (see Figure 5-28).
- Early reviews of the book, if any (see Figures 5-29 and 5-30).
- Response card (see Figure 5-31).
- Your touring calendar, if any.

"I am impressed with Marie Reichelt's book, *Yes, There Is Life After Aerospace* ... an excellent road map is required. Friends, here it is."

From the Foreword by Dick Rutan, Voyager Pilot.

Over 100,000 aerospace workers will be laid off this year alone ... they need this book!

A *Must Purchase* for Your Library!!

Dear Acquisition Librarian:

The statistics are horrifying! Over 100,000 aerospace workers will be laid off by the end of the year. This doesn't even include the 250,000 that have already lost their jobs.

California Hit Hardest — 1000s cut!

Thousands of Californians and others are losing their jobs every month. These ex-aerospace workers, as well as hundreds of military caught in the end-of-the-cold-war syndrome, are looking for ways to restart their lives and careers.

The First Book to Target Aerospace Workers in Years!!

YES, THERE IS LIFE AFTER AEROSPACE is the first book EVER WRITTEN to target the career transition plans of ex-aerospace and ex-military workers. Not just another rehash of generic "how to get a job" books. *Yes, There Is Life After Aerospace* talks to the aerospace and military personnel **in their language.**

Written by a Former Aerospace Human Resource Manager.

Written by former Human Resources Manager, Marie Hayashi Reichelt, herself a victim of a 1990 aerospace layoff, *YES, THERE IS LIFE AFTER*

AEROSPACE is written in simple, easy-to-understand prose that your patrons will like.

Foreword Written by Dick Rutan, Voyager Pilot.

"I am experienced with Marie Reichelt's book, *Yes, There Is Life After Aerospace.* It includes excellent guidance to those not used to dealing with the outside world. The reality is that we are now being forced to integrate, and for this integration to be successful, an excellent road map is required. Friends, here it is."

Here's What's Inside:

• What skills are really worth today
• Overcoming the stigma of defense work
• Assessing personal strengths for maximum impact
• Putting your financial house in order
• Handling interviews
• The unlisted job market
• Evaluating job offers
• Other options

Ordering Information for Libraries:

ISBN: 0-96390-365-9
LC: 94-07116
PUB DATE: September 15, 1994
PRICE: $14.95
SHIP DATE: Immediately
QUANTITY DISCOUNTS: See publ.

Order from: APB Publishers,
758 N. Quince Avenue, Upland, CA 91786 • (909) 982-7595

Figure 5-21. Promotional flyer targeted at acquisition librarians

REECE FRANKLIN & ASSOCIATES
14911 Rolling Ridge Drive
Chino Hills, CA 91709

(714) 393-8525

CONTACT: **Jeff Charlebois**
(818) 999-4623

**SIT-DOWN COMIC ROLLS ALONG WITH NEW BOOK LOOK AT MEDICAL
ESTABLISHMENT**

      (Woodland Hills, CA) -- Jeff Charlebois, America's Number 1 Sit-Down (Wheelchair-bound) comic, has published his new book "**MEDICAL SECRETS REVEALED: THE INSIDE SCOOP**." This tongue-in-cheek look at the medical profession covers "behind the scenes" truths, half-truths, and total hogwash about hospital medical antics.

      Charlebois spares no one—from naive candystripers (the backbone of an efficiently run hospital) to holier-than-thou surgeons (inside your editor—film at 11)—Jeff is able to take an irreverent look at what really happens from an insider's viewpoint.

      Since a car accident in 1979 left him paralyzed from the waist down, Jeff Charlebois has been crossing the country, using humor to talk about the "secrets known only by the hospital medical staff."

      Jeff's book reveals: what candystripers and Miss America contestants have in common; that nurses really _do_ like to give sponge baths; the three absolutely necessary traits of a good surgeon (skill isn't one of them).

      Charlebois is a well-known sit-down touring comic, and has performed at comedy clubs, colleges, rehab hospitals, and numerous medical functions (yes, they let him in again)! Jeff has been featured in over 100 newspapers and magazines.

      A former copywriter, Charlebois bills himself as a "ham on a roll." His motto is "where there's a wheel there's a way."

      Medical Secrets Revealed (ISBN 0-9641926-5-9) is 120 pages, paperbound, and retails for $14.95 ppd. For further information, or to book an interview, call Jeff directly at 818-999-4623.

#

MARKETING □ ADVERTISING □ PUBLIC RELATIONS

Figure 5-22. Sample news release, from book-review press kit (author's client)

Figure 5-23. Author's black-and-white studio portrait

AAJA Publishing Company

AUTHOR BIOGRAPHY

Reece Franklin is a small business consultant, specializing in marketing, advertising, and public relations for inventors and start ups.

He is an entrepreneur, lecturer, author, speaker, and trainer, and gives over 100 seminars and speeches annually.

Formerly, Reece owned Singman Publications, a trade specialty magazine company in San Diego. His production company, Franklin Television, produced three successful television shows, as well as two radio programs, one of which is still airing after six years.

He has been a fund raiser, executive director, trade show promoter; he owned his own public relations agency, and has even been a computer programmer.

But it has been his love of promotion, and helping the small businessman, that has been his sustenance. This caring has led to the authorship of his first major book, Inventor's Marketing Handbook: A Complete Guide to Selling and Promoting Your Invention. (AAJA Publishing Company, $19.95 postpaid).

In addition to this book, Franklin has published two small business monographs: 101 Ideas For News Releases, and Promotion and Sale Ideas for Retail Stores.

Just to make sure he doesn't get bored, Reece is premiering his new newsletter, Inventor's Almanac, at the Invention Convention in Pasadena, September 1 - 4. A quarterly companion piece to the marketing handbook, Inventor's Almanac is loaded with timely, helpful tips for the would-be invention marketer. In addition, Reece is helping to found the Inventor's Marketing Association, an independent organization for inventor cooperative marketing efforts.

P.O. Box 3694 La Habra, CA 90632-3694   (714) 526-6811

Figure 5-24.   Sample author biography, from a book-review press kit

If you were looking for an investor, you'd have to offer the same stock you hold—regular common stock—but you could reduce the recipient's voting rights. Since you're looking for an employee, it shouldn't be complicated. Peter Faber, a partner at Kaye, Scholer, Fierman, Hays & Handler, a New York City law firm, suggests offering not stock but a compensation arrangement with minimal salary and a percentage tied to the business's success.

"You don't want to give the employee a percentage of net profit," Faber says, because then the wisdom of your expenditures becomes an issue. Tie compensation to the gross minus the cost of goods sold, or, since you're hiring a salesperson, to sales. "If you get a person with an entrepreneurial spirit, the most attractive package will be something without guarantees but with a great up side if the business does well."

TURNING DREAMS INTO PROTOTYPES

I've developed a unit that removes fine particles from the air. It's been field-tested, and the Environmental Protection Agency wants a product proposal. That's no use if I can't take it to market. Are there companies that will see a concept through design and manufacturing, down to the end-user?

Stuart A. Hoenig
President
Associates in Applied Research
Tucson

You're wise to hold back: experts believe that of the quarter million patents sought annually, less than 5% prove commercially viable. Unfortunately, there's really no type of business that integrates design, prototype making, manufacturing, and marketing, says Tom Harlin, founder of Emergent Technologies, in Austin, Tex., who conducted a four-year study of invention marketing.

Get an industrial-design firm (IDF) to assess your blueprint and answer preliminary questions. Drew Santin, president of $4-million Santin Engineering, a product developer in Beverly, Mass. (see "Interacting with

Bankers [Revisited]," Banking and Capital, June), warns that IDFs range from one-man garages cranking out low-quality, $1,000 prototypes to larger outfits (with in-house consultants and access to manufacturing and consumer markets) asking as much as $20,000. Ultimately, cost boils down to how well you know your product and its market, and savvy negotiating skills don't hurt. Contact the Industrial Design Society of America (703-759-0100) for more information.

When the design is complete, an IDF typically consults a product developer like Santin, who identifies component flaws, generates ideas for packaging and strategic marketing, and targets end-users. Then you're ready to introduce the product at a trade show or contact large companies that might license it. (For more on licensing, see Royalty Treatment, July Network.)

The *Inventing and Patenting Sourcebook* (Gale Research, $79, 800-347-4253), available at research libraries, lists contacts at national, regional, and state agencies, on-line resources, and trade shows. It also offers specifics on 12,000 patent lawyers, 600 venture capitalists, and 100 big corporations that might be receptive to your patented technology. Reece Franklin's *Inventor's Marketing Handbook* (AAJA Publishing, $19.95, 170 pages, 714-393-8525) tells how to evaluate and name your product, file for a patent, size up the competition, assemble a press kit, and network at trade expos. Also, the Inventors Workshop International (IWI) offers consulting, referrals, seminars, and publications. IWI's annual InvenTech Expo brings together all interested parties. Call 805-484-9786 for information.

Reported by Michael P. Cronin, Karen E. Carney, Vera Gibbons, and Phaedra Hise.

Please send your words of advice to the Inc. Network, 38 Commercial Wharf, Boston, MA 02110, or call our answer response line, 800-238-1756. Or fax your letters to 617-248-8090. We'll publish the best responses and queries.

Figure 5-25. Single clip sheet reprint from author's press kit. © *Reprinted with permission of* Inc. *Magazine, 1992.*

Author Available For Interviews

My students tell me . . .

> my seminars are the most "hands-on", down to earth they've ever taken.

Radio interviewers have said . . .

> "one of the best shows I've done in a long time. The four hours flew by, with stimulating questions and answers."

> "Really knows what he's talking about. Hard-hitting facts straight to the inventor."

Television interviewers have said . . .

> "Excellent shows. Very visual and fun to do. Wide variety of products makes good television."

> "Great show. Smooth, free-flowing segment."

Newspaper reporters say I make it easy for them.

Who is this man, and why are they talking about him like this?

I'm a former editor and broadcaster who knows the ins and outs of the profession and what you're looking for in a quality interview.

I know what makes good television, a stimulating radio interview, and a thought-provoking feature story. I offer these to you, along with my expertise on invention marketing, a most stimulating subject.

Did you know, for example, that over 98% of the inventions patented in the United States NEVER make it to market?

In my book, INVENTOR'S MARKETING HANDBOOK, I've solved that problem for the inventor.

And I can solve problems for your listeners, viewers, and readers.

I will be available for interviews on the following dates:

Baltimore - Thursday, May 17
Washington, DC and Virginia - Wed. And Fri., May 16 and 18

Let's get together and make the phones and letters pour in.

Reece Franklin   **714-393-8525**

Figure 5-26. Sample author available sheet, from a book-review press kit

REECE FRANKLIN & ASSOCIATES
14911 Rolling Ridge Drive
Chino Hills, CA 91709

(714) 393-8525

REVIEWER'S FACT SHEET

MEDICAL SECRETS REVEALED: THE INSIDE SCOOP

Pub Date: Sept. 1   ISBN: 0-96419-265-9

Ship Date: Aug. 1   Pages: 118   Price: $14.95

Glossary, Index, Illustrations

BLURB

Medical Secrets Revealed: The Inside Scoop, is the
hilariously funny not-so-true-to-life scenes behind the average
hospital stay. For anyone who's ever been a patient, or had the
patience to receive medical attention, this book is the constant
reference to the insane world of medicine, doctors, and hospitals.

Author Jeff Charlebois, a wheelchair-bound comic, takes a very
tongue-in-cheek look at the medical world of doctors, nurses, X-ray
technicians, urologists (ouch!), surgeons, OTs and PTs, using his
real-life experiences as examples of the "Mad, Mad, Mad World of
Medicine."

Table of Contents

Candy Stripers
Nurses
X-Ray Technicians
Urologists
Anesthesiologists
Surgeons
Physical Therapists
Occupational Therapists
Maintenance Men

PUBLICITY PLANS

Author College Lecture and Sit-Down Comic Tour - Fall, 1995
Articles - Challenge and Disability Magazines
Radio Publicity
Major Tie In With Disability Month
Selected Author Tour - Bookstores

Le Bois Productions, 5807 Topanga Canyon Blvd., Suite G-309
Woodland Hills, CA 91367 (818) 999-4623

Figure 5-27.   Sample reviewer's fact sheet from a book-review
press kit

AAJA PUBLISHING COMPANY
14911 Rolling Ridge Drive
Chino Hills, CA 91709
714-393-8525

Sample Questions for Reece Franklin Interview

1. Who invents these products?

2. What traits make a successful inventor?

3. How many inventions actually see the marketplace?

4. What are the two main problems inventors face?

5. Why are you lobbying Congress for National Inventor's Day?

6. What about invention marketing companies?

7. You say patents are not necessarily helpful? Why not?

8. How can an inventor find a manufacturer to sell to?

9. How does one sell to the government?

10. What are the three key questions any inventor should ask?

11. What's an ideal product?

12. When should the inventor begin to think about marketing?

Figure 5-28. Sample Q-&-A for radio, TV interviews, from author's book-review press kit

How to market your business and stay home

Chino man's latest book could have the answers

By Nicholas Wadhams
For the Daily Bulletin

CHINO — Reece Franklin is a realist.

In his latest book, "How To Market Your Home-Based Business," he writes that starting a home-based business is "time-consuming, frustrating and many other not-so-nice adjectives."

But Franklin also knows it can be very rewarding – and he wants to help small- business owners find success of their own.

A marketing and advertising consultant since 1988, Franklin helps to shape up business images with techniques he's learned since his start in 1972, when he helped raise funds for numerous health and community organizations in Illinois.

In addition to writing, Franklin teaches more than 80 classes and seminars a year, sells audiotapes of his concepts, and offers business evaluations. "I'm one big marketing information company with many different hats," he said.

Franklin's new book is no Charles Dickens novel. Filling a little more than 100 pages, it is written simply and pumps out information in short bites. It details everything from licensing and red tape to effective letterhead design.

Franklin describes the self-published book as a guide to the "nuts and bolts" of marketing a home-based business.

He said he tried to write the book in his teaching style – full of sarcasm and exclamation points to keep his readers interested. In fact, the book is a condensed version of his classes, he said, and was written primarily for students who wanted more than their own quickly scribbled notes.

"How To Market Your Home-Based Business" is Franklin's second book. In 1990, he self-published "The Inventor's Marketing Handbook," which sold around 4,000 copies.

Franklin said he has already received a publishing commitment for a third book he is preparing to write, "The Consultant's Guide to Public Relations." The book will be published by John Wiley and Sons of New York City.

Walt Weis/Daily Bulletin
Teacher-author Reece Franklin's latest book is entitled "How To Market Your Home-Based Business."

He is proud of his pending move to a publishing house. "It's hard for a self-publisher to get in with the big guys," he said.

Still, Franklin's biggest concern right now is "How To Market Your Home-Based Business," which is still in the prototype stage, with only 350 copies printed. He said he has high hopes for the book because its release coincides with California's slow emergence from a long period of recession.

Franklin said he hopes the book will benefit small-business owners who are struggling just as he did when he founded his marketing firm.

"If I can teach someone something and they do a little bit better, that makes me feel good," he said.

Figure 5-29. Book review reprint, from a book-review press kit

96

AAJA PUBLISHING COMPANY
P O BOX 2667
CHINO, CA 91708-2667
714-393-8525

WHAT OTHERS HAVE SAID ABOUT US...

Franklin, Reece A. **Inventor's Marketing Handbook: A Complete Guide to Selling and Promoting Your Invention.**
AAJA Pub. Co. 1989. 175p. bibliog. index. LC 89-85370. ISBN 0-9623938-7-8. pap. $19.95. BUS
This is a general introduction to marketing inventions aimed at individuals who already have been awarded a patent. Obviously based on the author's marketing seminar, this easy-to-read handbook will appeal to both the new and experienced inventor as much for the lists of questions inventors should ask as for the lists of do's and don't's. Strengths include its currency, its coverage of advertising, and its relative uniqueness among the piles of how-to books in patenting. It has a short bibliography and no footnotes, but it does include a very large number of both book and organizational resources in the text. Public libraries will find this a quite acceptable purchase.—*Patrick J. Brunet, Univ. of Wisconsin Lib., La Crosse*

LIBRARY JOURNAL/JANUARY 1990

THE BLOOMSBURY REVIEW—March/April 1990

Inventor's Marketing Handbook
A Complete Guide to Selling and Promoting Your Invention
REECE A. FRANKLIN
AAJA *Publishing*, $19.95 *paper*,
ISBN 0-962-3938-7-8; Box 3694,
La Habra, CA 90631

I encourage would-be inventors to read this book *before* they begin to spend much time or money on designing their widget. Most inventions succeed because of marketing, regardless of how wonderful or useful to society the idea is. If you have plans to make your inventing career more than an expensive hobby, marketing might be the most important part of your job. I found the tips on analyzing who might buy your invention particularly valuable.   —PW

Figure 5-30. Sample clip sheet with early reviews, from a book-review press kit

PLEASE ACKNOWLEDGE

We have received your News Release about **Inventor's Marketing Handbook**

We will take the following action:

____ Your book will be featured on (date): _____
____ Your book will be featured in the near future.
____ Please send a photo of the book.
____ Please send a complimentary copy of the book.

Name: _____
Full job title: _____
Name of publication or broadcast station: _____
Mailing address: _____
_____ Zip: _____
Comments (opt.): _____
_____

Figure 5-31. Sample response card, from a book-review press kit

SUMMARY

For your convenience, Table 5-5 gives an overview of the items appropriate for each type of press kit.

SUMMARY

Table 5-5.   Press Kit Comparison Chart

ITEM	TYPE			
	BASIC	EXPANDED	SPEAKER'S	BOOK REV.
Articles about you		Yes	Yes	Yes
Articles about other books				Yes
Articles by you (reprints)		Yes	Yes	
Author touring calendar				Yes
Biography	Yes	Yes	Yes	Yes
Book brochure or flyer		Yes	Yes	Yes
Book covers, extra (in folder)				Yes
Book reviews, early			Yes	Yes
Case history		Yes		
Clip sheet, electronic	Yes	Yes	Yes	
Clip sheet, print		Yes	Yes	Yes
Contract, copy of			Yes	
Cover letter			Yes	Yes
Demo tape, audio (live)			Yes	
Demo tape, video (live)			Yes	Yes
Fact sheet	Yes	Yes		
Fee schedule			Yes	
List of happy clients		Yes	Yes	
Menu of services offered				Yes
News release	Yes	Yes	Yes	Yes
One-sheet flyer			Yes	
Op-ed piece		Yes		
Personal backgrounder	Yes	Yes	Yes	Yes
Photo of client (action)	Yes	Yes	Yes	
Photo of you (head shot)	Yes	Yes	Yes	Yes
Practice brochure		Yes	Yes	
Q-and-A sample (broadcast)		Yes	Yes	Yes
Testimonial letters		Yes	Yes	
Topic title and outline			Yes	

CHAPTER 6

Tools of the Trade— Additional Documents You Need

There are many publicity tools you need to know about as a consultant. Some are right for every situation, some not. Let's discuss each one and how and where it fits into the scheme of things.

THE SAVVY CONSULTANT'S PUBLICITY TOOLS—ALL THE "DOCS" YOU NEED TO KNOW

For the smart consultant, it's not just "Take one tool, and see your story in the morning news!" You must take advantage of all the opportunities for publicity today—or even make those opportunities happen—by being prepared and learning how to use the following 25 tools.

1. News release.
2. Media advisory.

3. Public-service announcement (PSA).
4. Company backgrounder.
5. Fact sheet.
6. Case history.
7. Op-ed piece.
8. Letter to the editor.
9. Featurette.
10. Feature article.
11. Photo.
12. Question-and-answer.
13. Newsletter.
14. Event.
15. Speech.
16. Seminar.
17. Teaching.
18. Clip sheet—print.
19. Electronic contact sheet.
20. TV talk show.
21. Radio talk show.
22. Cable TV show.
23. Trade show.
24. Book or booklet, and audiotape.
25. Video news release.

General Rules for Most Documents

The general rules for most documents you'll need to create are:

1. Print on letterhead.
2. Double-space—use one side of paper only.
3. Provide contact name(s) at the top left.
4. Put contact phone number(s) at the top left, under the name.

5. Include a release date—"For release on MM/DD/YY" or "For immediate release."

Try not to have multiple-page releases or any documents longer than two pages. It's just not cricket to expect any journalist to wade through volumes of paper in order to determine the key points in your story. They'll throw the whole thing out.

News Release

This is the core element we discussed in Chapter 5. From this will flow articles, feature stories, and other documents written by you, or by the media itself. The news release will always be the first element you put together in a publicity campaign. And it's the first item you send to the press when you have a new story idea. Make sure you understand how to write it and when to send it. (If not, go back and reread Chapter 5.)

Media Advisory

You use the media advisory to give advance information about an upcoming event you might be producing, such as a speech or seminar, or about one you will appear in, like a small-business conference. The media advisory is sent to the assignment editors of television news, news directors at radio stations, and the correct contact reporter/editor at your local and regional publications.

The format uses the standard five-Ws-and-H formula you learned in Chapter 5. In fact, I boldface the who-what-where-when-why-and-how, list it along the left side, and then fill in the blanks. It makes it easy for an assignment editor or reporter to see exactly what's occurring and when. And the easier you make it for them, the more coverage you'll get.

The media advisory is similar to the basic press kit fact sheet. The difference is when it is sent—one month earlier.

Figure 6-1 shows a typical media advisory. Notice the How row is the biggest. That's the key. Telling the media exactly how their coverage will benefit their readers, viewers, or listeners will help you zero in on them.

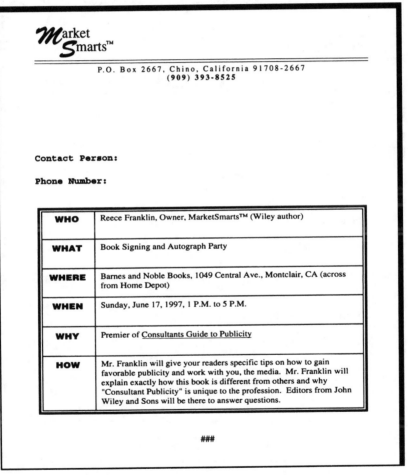

Market Smarts™

P.O. Box 2667, Chino, California 91708-2667
(909) 393-8525

Contact Person:

Phone Number:

WHO	Reece Franklin, Owner, MarketSmarts™ (Wiley author)
WHAT	Book Signing and Autograph Party
WHERE	Barnes and Noble Books, 1049 Central Ave., Montclair, CA (across from Home Depot)
WHEN	Sunday, June 17, 1997, 1 P.M. to 5 P.M.
WHY	Premier of Consultants Guide to Publicity
HOW	Mr. Franklin will give your readers specific tips on how to gain favorable publicity and work with you, the media. Mr. Franklin will explain exactly how this book is different from others and why "Consultant Publicity" is unique to the profession. Editors from John Wiley and Sons will be there to answer questions.

###

Figure 6-1. Sample media advisory

Public-Service Announcement

The public-service announcement, or PSA, is normally used with not-for-profit organizations, associations, and charities, not with businesses. Figure 6-2 illustrates the general format a PSA uses. The only way for you as a consultant to get a PSA to work for you is to tie in with a charity or be a member of any association and

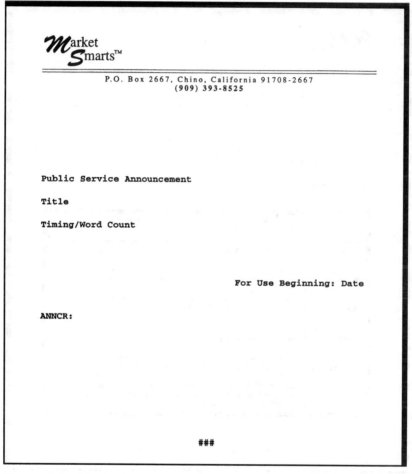

Figure 6-2. Public-service announcement one-pager format to use with your letterhead

then donate something of value (like time, money, services) to them. Let the charity send out the release and/or PSA, which includes mention of you.

To see how to create one, look at Figure 6-3, which shows the PSA for the California Society of Enrolled Agents (CSEA). (Figure 6-2 is a blank PSA form to show the basic format.) The story behind

P.O. Box 2667, Chino, California 91708-2667
(909) 393-8525

PUBLIC SERVICE ANNOUNCEMENT

"CSEA TIPS FOR SAVING TAXES"

60 SECS/ 100 WORDS

For Use Beginning March 1, 1993

ANNCR: MARCH IS TAX AWARENESS MONTH. BE SURE TO TAKE
EVERY DEDUCTION YOU POSSIBLY CAN. ACCORDING TO THE
CALIFORNIA SOCIETY OF ENROLLED AGENTS, OVER 60% OF TAX
FILERS DO NOT TAKE ALL THE DEDUCTIONS THEY'RE ALLOWED.
THE IRS LOVES THIS. ACCORDING TO CSEA, THIS GIVES THE
FEDS A WINDFALL OF OVER $3 BILLION DOLLARS PER TAX YEAR.
SO BE SURE TO ITEMIZE. AND GET HELP FROM AN ENROLLED
AGENT, LICENSED TO PRACTICE BEFORE THE IRS.

A PUBLIC SERVICE MESSAGE OF THE CALIFORNIA SOCIETY OF
ENROLLED AGENTS, SAN BERNARDINO CHAPTER.

###

Figure 6-3. Sample public-service announcement for California Society of Enrolled Agents

the PSA in Figure 6-3 begins with Glenn Duncan, my tax man and an enrolled agent who is currently the CSEA chapter vice president in San Bernardino/Riverside, CA. (An *enrolled agent* is not a CPA but is licensed to practice and represent you before the Internal Revenue Service.)

In January 1993, Glenn asked me to speak before his chapter on marketing and publicity for small businesses. (Enrolled agents are all independent business owners and consultants.)

During the speech, which was in and of itself a publicity tool I use frequently, I mentioned PSAs. After dinner, Glenn and several others discussed the possibility of enhancing their image through PSAs. I told them I'd be delighted to help out and quoted my fee. (This is a way for you to work the aftermarket sales of your services as well.)

We agreed I'd produce four 60-second PSAs for the chapter. These would be generic, so that any other chapter could pick them up and use them, thus offsetting his chapter's costs.

Figure 6-3 is one of a series of four 60-second PSAs. Notice how the format is different. Here we tell the radio or television personnel that it's a PSA. We give it a title, and note the length and approximate word count (rounding off to nearest 25). We also tell them when we want them to use it. In this case, since it is about taxes, the timing was crucial. I didn't want it to run prior to March 1, even though it was produced and sent in early February. Why? People don't think about taxes until that time. Finally, notice that we show the announcer where to start his or her patter.

By the way, you can say about 20 words in ten seconds, so your starting point for a "sixty" will be about 120 words. Then you'll probably cut down from there, depending on the number of multi-syllable words you have. It's best to time it out.

A cautionary note: Since you're never sure what an announcer will do to your script, or how they'll read it, it's important to make your own tape of the spot and send it with the written version. That way you can emphasize exactly the words you want stressed.

Never assume the station announcer will guess how you want it read.

By the way, double-space the announcement and—only for this type of tool—capitalize the words.

How did we place the enrolled-agent PSAs? After sending them to all San Bernardino and Riverside County radio stations and to selected Los Angeles basin ones, like KNX and KFWB news radio, I followed up with phone calls to the stations' public service directors. If they didn't have one, I asked who was in charge of PSAs.

Results? Three stations in our area used several of them, and a reporter from KFWB interviewed Glenn (since his name was the contact name on the PSA.) Total investment for the chapter— $3,000 for my fee and production. (I found a good audio studio during off-hours, taped the spots myself to save announcer fees, and duplicated the masters at an inexpensive dupe house instead of the studio.) Each member of the chapter paid $20 for his/her share. Glenn then assigned any inquiries to the member who was nearest the radio listener. Several members got new clients—a bonus. More important, the chapter got great publicity. Success breeds success, they say!

How did *I* get publicity? In this case I'm not mentioned in the PSA. That's OK. The feedback and results generated new business for me through word-of-mouth. The other way to use a PSA? Write one gratis for a charity, and let them send it out with your name added.

Company Backgrounder

While most media consultants call any position paper that explains your stand on an issue a "backgrounder," I believe there is a distinct difference between a position paper, or *white paper,* and the simple one-page backgrounder that you'll need. To me, a position paper is a long drawn-out rewording of technobabble that no reporter or editor wants to read.

In contrast, a simple, one-page, doublespaced backgrounder that gives the who, what, where, when, why, and how is what you want. It's very helpful to the media because it gives them extra information they can use to flesh out a story. A sample backgrounder appears in Figure 6-4.

FREEDOM TO FLY

COMPANY BACKGROUNDER

FREEDOM TO FLY$_{tm}$

What: FREEDOM TO FLY$_{tm}$ is a seminar and taped program company specializing in helping travelers overcome their fear of flying.

Who: Ralph Tassinari, Ph.D.
Licensed psychologist
Adjunct faculty, USC
Co-founder, FREEDOM TO FLY$_{tm}$

Mr. Roger Martin
First Officer, United Airlines
Co-founder, FREEDOM TO FLY$_{tm}$

Where: Home office - 27871 Medical Center Rd., Ste. 285
Mission Viejo, CA 92691

When: Founded November, 1988.

Why: Over 45 million American travelers are afraid to fly. The level of this fear ranges from mild anxiety to one so strong that some people won't fly at all. FREEDOM TO FLY was established to help these people overcome their fears so that they can be free to travel like everyone else.

How: Audio tapes, video tapes, seminars, lectures.

Contact: Shirley Lashmett, Marketing Director
(800) 635-6648

###

Figure 6-4. Sample company backgrounder, a one-pager using the five-*W*s-and-*H* format plus a contact line (put on your company's letterhead)

Fact Sheet

The fact sheet is a spec sheet on each service you offer. Again, a simple, one-page, one-sided who-what-where-etc. gives a reporter or editor the essentials. Many a time I've prepared a fact sheet based on a release and then talked to a very happy reporter who said, "I really appreciate how easy you made it for me to find the crucial facts in a sheet I could skim. I get so many releases per day, it's nice to have someone lay it out for me. No clutter, no waste."

So should you just repeat the release in the fact sheet, with a different format? No, the release is written in story form, with full sentences, quotes, facts, and anecdotes to explain the five Ws. The fact sheet is a brief here-it-is. I liken it to any outline sheet for a release. In fact, you could do the fact sheet first, writing in the who, what, and so on and then convert it to the release. It might be easier for you that way. Try it both ways, though, to start. First release, then fact sheet, then vice versa. You'll get a feel for what's comfortable.

For those of you with actual hard products like books, tapes, videos, and so on, you'll create a fact sheet for your product media kit, as discussed in the last chapter. For selling consulting services a similar format, but with different fill-ins, will be used. Figures 6-5 and 6-6 show you the formats for both product and consulting fact sheets.

Case History

A case history is a short, one- to two-page summary of a client's problem and how you solved it. This tool is used more for marketing purposes than for publicity, but it can be added to a press kit to show specific industry examples of how you are the "consummate professional and expert."

Start a case history with the problem, then discuss the options that were available. Finish with the solution you took and why. The

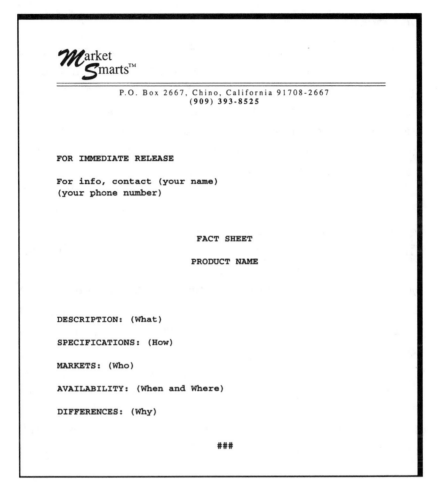

Figure 6-5. Product fact sheet format, to use with your letterhead

end product is similar to a short-form consultant's proposal (see Ron Tepper's *The Consultant's Proposal, Fee, and Contract Problem Solver,* published by John Wiley and Sons).

Op-ed Piece

The op-ed piece is a more sophisticated tool, but one that can give you tremendous exposure. It is, in effect, a guest column, run op-

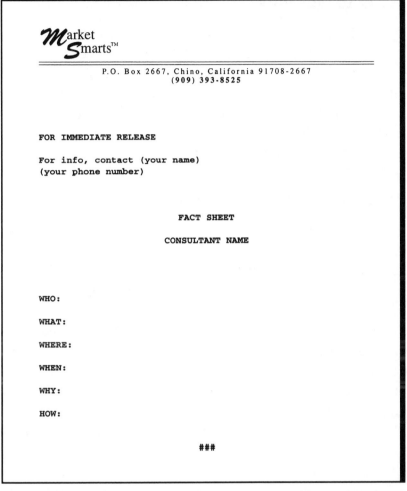

Figure 6-6. Consulting fact sheet format, to use with your letterhead

posite the editorial page of a newspaper or magazine. It may or may not relate to previous opinions of the publication.

Most op-ed pieces are written by syndicated columnists, so your chances for space are small. However, with a well-written piece and good credentials (the press lately seems to love women and academics), you may be able to get one in.

Letter to the Editor

Writing a letter to the editor is a relatively easy way to get into the press. Most publications offer their readers a chance to sound off about one thing or another. Make sure you keep your letter brief (about 150 words) and directly to the point. Don't ramble. Tightly edit your writing. And be sure to include your name, company name, and city at the bottom. Too many letters show name and city, but no company name. What a waste of good PR space!

Featurette and Feature Article

Here's where the smart consultant stands out from the crowd. Develop a 750-word-short featurette about your consulting. Be sure to weave in plenty of examples from real clients. Discuss how you have solved client problems and how your solutions apply to current social problems.

The featurette is usually a one-shot deal, although if you do it right, you might wind up with a series. One of my clients, a human resources specialist, was approached by the publisher of our local regional newspaper to do a series on how to get a job during the recession. Obviously, timing is sometimes everything.

Whatever you do, there's always use for your articles later on, as seminar handouts or as submissions to other publications around the country. This is called *self-syndication*.

Feature articles are longer, between 1,500 and 3,000 words. Normally most newspapers won't run these. However, you may find a home for them among trade and business publications.

The List Article. The simplest type of article to write is the *list article*. This is a series of steps that guide the reader into doing something. For our financial-planner consultants, it might be "Ten Steps to Retirement at 50." The first article, or the overview, would give the top nine general steps. Didn't I say "10"? Of course. But step 10 is always Buy Me. Here's a sample:

Step 1. Put together a goal for the future.

Step 2. Check all available assets you have.

Step 3. Check all liabilities you have.

Step 4. Take each asset and study it in light of the economic, political, and social aspects of what futurists are predicting.

Step 5. Take this data, make a card for each asset, and prioritize the assets.

You get the idea, don't you? And step 10, the "buy me"? Here's one: "Have a seasoned financial planner go over your game plan with you to find any holes." (That's, of course, you.)

At the bottom of the article, include what Dr. Jeffrey Lant calls a *resource box.* That's the area where you put your name, address, phone number, and other pertinent data so the reader can buy you.

For example, here's the sort of thing I might put in a resource box:

> Reece Franklin is the owner of MarketSmarts, a Chino-based full-service advertising and publicity company. He's the author of "Consultant's Guide to Publicity" by John Wiley and Sons. For a free copy of his report "101 Ideas for Press Releases," write to him at P.O. Box 2667, Chino, CA 91708-2667, or telephone (909) 393-8525.

Sixty percent of the editors either will not run the resource box or will edit it substantially. But that leaves a full 40 percent who will. And the way I write it, with an offer to the readers of a *free* report, increases the chances of it getting printed. Even if my address and phone number are left out, guess what? Reece Franklin is listed in the Chino phone book. So prospects who really want me, find me. (And many have.)

By the way, several times I've had my articles run verbatim by editors, including the full resource box. It makes it all worthwhile!

Photo

Photos should be used to supplement your release or be sent by themselves with caption sheets (called *stand-alone* photos). Whenever you send a release, ALWAYS SEND A PHOTO. A good photo can save a mediocre release. Remember, a picture is worth a thousand words. Type a caption, double-spaced, at the bottom of a sheet of plain white bond. Attach it to the back of the photo with tape. Do *not* write on the back of the photo.

What's a good caption? A simple, one-sentence "who it is and what's it all about." Nothing else.

Photos should be action photos. No one likes the boring, standard shot of two people passing checks back and forth. If you have more than three people in a photo, most editors don't want it.

Make sure you put your client, as well as yourself, in the photo. Also ask, Is it a good action shot? Does it show what you did for the client, his products, or service? Can you show the product or service moving or working?

The only time you want a mug shot is when you're doing an article. In that case, send in a bust shot (from the chest up) with your article(s) (see Chapter 5 for author's photo).

In all cases, photos should be QUALITY. Please don't take them yourself or hire your brother-in-law. For the bust shot, hire a fashion photographer to make you look your best. Face facts, friends—not everyone is photogenic. But a good fashion photographer (and perhaps airbrush artist) can do wonders. Why go to all the expense? It's your image, folks.

Photos must be 4 × 6 or 5 × 7 black-and-white glossies. Have at least a dozen poses taken, and have someone with a critical eye pick the best one. Then find a photo-duplication house in the Yellow Pages, check prices, and have them make up at least 300 prints. Believe me, with the campaign you'll do, you'll need them.

Here on the West Coast, I use a company called Photomation, based in Anaheim, CA. They're very reasonable, about 38 cents a pix. And they deliver for free. They deal with many publicists and all the major Hollywood studios, so I know they're good. (Their address is in Appendix 7 if you want to use them. Tell them I sent you.)

Question-and-Answer

You'll use question-and-answers (Q-and-As) normally only with electronic media for news interviews and talk shows. The pressure of deadlines in broadcast media is much greater than in newspapers. Broadcasters live by the minute, print people by the day. So a Q-and-A format is very helpful to TV and radio people. (Print people often feel that any Q-and-A is telling them how to write, which they already know.)

Since broadcasters, especially talk-show hosts, are so harassed, it's possible—and highly likely—that the questions and answers you send in will be read verbatim over the air. The whole purpose of the Q-and-A is to get broadcasters to ask you questions you're prepared to answer so you look like the expert you are.

Here are the types of questions I'd prepare in advance of any TV or radio interview. I'd send them in a press kit, after the show producer had gotten my initial release and shown interest (see Chapter 5).

Q1. Why did you write this book?
Q2. How is consultant publicity different from product publicity?
Q3. Can anyone use these techniques?
Q4. What are some of your success stories? (My clients, of course.)

You see how it works? Now, why not try to outline a few questions of your own for that upcoming talk-show host.

By the way, you may be asking, "How do I know when to send the press kit, Reece? And how do I get them to accept the Q-and-A format?" Good questions.

You send the press kit when they ask you for more information, not before. If they don't ask, don't send. That's why the release had better work hard for you. I never spend money sending out press kits to people who don't want them. Neither should you. Be frugal—even downright cheap. It's money.

Once I've sent the release, I follow up with a call to the talk-show producer or assignment editor or planner to discuss a possible interview about my story. After we've discussed my sending a press kit with the further information, so they can get a better feel for what a great guest I am, I'll say, "Would it be all right if I send you several of the most-often-asked questions for these types of interviews, so you and your host can get a feel for what's happening?" I've never been turned down yet.

What you're doing is stacking the deck. Send them twelve good questions that cover *everything* important about you, your company, and your clients. Since you'll be able to rattle off the answers, you'll look good and become the instant, accessible expert. (Be sure to bring a copy of the Q-and-A with you to the interview.)

I once had a radio host, for an entire hour, ask all dozen questions from a sheet, verbatim. The station was in the western U.S.; I was at home in Chino Hills, being interviewed long distance (see "TV and Radio Talk Shows" later in this chapter). My wife happened to be with a friend in San Diego. Since the station had 50,000 watts, they could hear it 300 miles or more away.

The host asked me the same 12 questions I've used for years (this was on my first book, *Inventor's Marketing Handbook,* AAJA, 1989). He read them straight from the sheet, and every ten minutes or so he said, "Now, what was that 800 number so my listeners can order the book, Reece?" Later, my wife asked me if he was on our payroll, he did such a selling job. Sixty minutes of national air time pitching Reece's book. (It doesn't always happen like that, folks, but it can if you try.)

Newsletter

In past years I would have advocated putting together a simple, one- or two-page newsletter, two-sided, with black-plus-one-color ink. And for certain types of businesses, that's still viable. However, because so many consultants and others are doing newsletters, it's become old hat. My recommendation now is to take that same newsletter information, write it the same way—short, punchy, full of tidbits of information—but reformat it into a three- or four-page letter. Not a sales type of letter with a headline or Johnson box (like you find in direct-mail letters) at the top, but a chitchatty letter, written as if to a friend. It's almost like a conversational letter full of case histories. These seem to pull much better than newsletters, as long as they're not boring.

How long should they be? Long enough to tell short snippets of wisdom your clients can use but not so long they bore. Use plenty of case histories. If you find yourself repeating a point more than once, reedit and rewrite.

Event

While we don't want to use publicity stunts without any substance behind them just to gain attention, event publicity does have its place. Where? Launching your book is one venue; a major speech attacking something that can harm your clients might be another.

What exactly, then, is an *event?*

It's a well-thought-out, highly staged publicity happening that's part of an overall campaign. For example, when I launched my first book on invention marketing, I knew I needed a way to gain attention yet still carry some credibility. The old-fashioned way of doing a "stunt" would brand me as a publicity hound. Oh, sure, the media would've eaten it up, whatever it was. But my long-range goal of being recognized as an expert in invention marketing would have been damaged irreparably. At the same time, I needed to get the book massive visibility. Quite a conundrum.

One problem—that same fall of 1989, three other books on invention marketing were coming out. So, how was I going to pull off an event and get people to want the book?

Part of the problem was solved when I learned of the Invention Convention held every year at the Pasadena Civic Center on Labor Day. I bought a booth for $500 and ordered four or five boxes of books, shipped directly from the printer to the Center.

In talking to the trade-show promoter, I learned that, yes indeed, other books were being launched there.

I asked the promotor if he knew the type of display booths the other authors had, and he assured me they were standard, not out of the ordinary, strictly legit. Good, I thought, I'll bend the rules a little. Here's how I did it.

First, I noted that inventors need to learn how to market their new products—and, hey, I'm a marketer.

Second, I determined that the other authors were inventors, not marketers. They were likely to approach the show from an academic viewpoint, at best.

Third, I observed that I share a last name, Franklin, with that well-known inventor Ben Franklin. What's more, he was also a publisher and writer. I'm a self-published author.

Putting it all together, I decided to dress as Ben Franklin and get attention. Result: I sold more books that weekend than any other author there. Moreover, I got the publicity I wanted. Almost every TV crew and radio station stopped by to find out what was going on. And I booked two radio interviews for that month.

Would I do it again? You bet! Sometimes, dear consultants, you have to get NOTICED!

Other Types of Event.   What other staged events can you be part of yet still maintain dignity? Well, anything that ties in with your ongoing community involvement, like the Chamber of Commerce Expo, or a Business-to-Business Conference.

How about a local charity auction where you donate one hour of FREE Consulting? That'll work. Be sure to sit down with the auctioneer or executive director ahead of time to explain exactly what someone wins, item by item, so the value is announced correctly. (It might help to write your own introduction to your donation so they get it right.)

If you're still stuck for ideas on types of events consultants can do, find a copy of *Chase's Annual Events* in your local library. This lists every major event in North America, day by day throughout the year. Reading through the listings will help you spin off new ideas.

Speech and Lecture

Speeches and lectures are relatively inexpensive but not easy to do. Use the *Encyclopedia of Associations* regional editions to find lists of local Chambers, Rotary Clubs Kiwanis Clubs, Lions Club, Elks, and other fraternal and community associations and groups to speak to.

What's a good speech topic? How about converting that ten-step list article into a dynamite talk of 30 to 40 minutes? Start with a powerful opener, use the middle to talk about the ten steps, and close with "you can do it too, and I'll help you."

Make a list of whom you wish to speak to, according to the objectives, strategies, and tactics mentioned in earlier chapters. Again, for a dynamite book on setting up a speaking career, or just to learn the basics, I recommend Dottie Walter's *Speak and Grow Rich*.

Seminar and Workshop

Planning and intense preparation is required for a seminar or workshop. Yet just one can yield great contacts and possible buyers. (For a complete guide to putting on seminars, get Gordon Burgett's *How to Set Up and Market Your Own Seminar;* you can order directly from Communication Unlimited, P.O. Box 6405, Santa Maria, CA 93456.) Seminars are either self-sponsored or sponsored by an outside organization. They're daylong affairs, expensive to produce and execute. Don't try self-sponsored ones unless you have deep pockets.

Workshops and teaching, on the other hand, are low-risk. They are school-sponsored, which means that the schools pay for limited promotion and list you within a catalog mailed to thousands of local residents and businesses. You must, however, do your own outside publicity. The schools simply don't have adequate marketing budgets.

Most of my previous clients have come from workshops I conduct at various community and four-year colleges throughout Southern California. Here's how I get them.

I pack into four short hours everything basic I think adult learners need to know about a certain subject. In fact, the only criticism I ever get is "too much stuff in too little time." I do this on purpose. About hour three, they realize there is a lot to this. When they say, "Whew! That's a lot of stuff to have to accomplish. Can you help? Do you do consulting?" I gladly reply, "Of course I do."

Note: you don't want to make the four hours so simple that they think it's a pitch for your consulting services. Many schools balk at letting you give out your business card. So be careful. If asked, just quietly say, "I can talk about that during the break." Same thing with fees—hold answers until break time.

Clip Sheet—Print

As we saw in Chapter 5, the clip sheet is a page with copies of articles that have already been published, either by you or about you. Take the three most recent articles printed about you or your products or service. Reproduce them on your letterhead, on one side only, along with the name, day, and date of the publication at the top, and send them with your press kit.

If the articles are too long, reproduce just the paragraph before and after your are mentioned, and circle your name. In all cases, make sure the headline and date are also reproduced.

Use the clip sheet to show credibility. Prove that you know the rules. Prove that you've been in print before.

Electronic Contact Sheet

While it's not possible to send copies of broadcast news and interviews, you can send an electronic contact sheet, a list of the stations and dates you were interviewed. On your letterhead, list the station call letters (KABC, for example), date you appeared, name of program, producer, host, and city and state.

TV and Radio Talk Shows

Talk shows get sophisticated and are some of the most impressive tools you can use. Doing your own talk show can be very rewarding and bring you lots of publicity, but the task of doing one, week after week, for thirteen weeks (the normal time sequence TV and radio stations demand) can be brutal. And it's very costly. I know. I've produced six of them on local cable. My advice is to start by booking yourself as a guest on local interview shows until you're a master at working with the camera or radio equipment—and, of course, the interviewer (see Chapter 8, "Setting Up Interviews").

In terms of the big boys—Oprah, Geraldo, Phil, and the others—we consultants need to face facts. Unless you have something so outrageous or so unique that the producers come begging you "to come on," most of the time it won't happen. (Exception to the rule: anything dealing with psychology, if it's a new twist, might get you booked.) The reality is, those big shows are looking for controversy, hype, and anything else to get those rating points, ergo advertising revenues, up. My advice—forget it!

Cable Television.   Within each community in the United States, different cable companies are licensed to lay cable and feed broadcasts through the system. Most of the country is now hooked up with cable. Each community cable company is charged with the responsibility for providing both regular programming and local origination channel (LOC) programming. The regular programming they get from cable producers and networks like CNN, Lifestyle, Discovery, the Disney Channel, and so on. The local programming they get from you!

LOC Programming.   LOC programming usually involves city council meetings, church plays, community theater, and the like. However, the enterprising consultant can make great use of this for his or her publicity campaign (if the target audience is the local community).

Federal Communications Commission rules state that *every* cable carrier *must* carry a certain amount of local programming. You, as a local community consultant, can make sure they do their job. Call up the carrier and ask for the person in charge of the local programming. Ask them if they have a local talk show. If so, how do you get on? If not, start your own. They'll help you—up to a point. You must provide your own crew, however. Then there's scripting, sets, guests to interview, and so on. It can be very time consuming. If you have the time, you can tape three or four shows in one day, so you only come in once a month.

By the way, the cost is practically nothing. As long as you don't sell commercials or blatantly advertise your consulting services, the cable company will provide the studio, tape, and one producer free. The rest you do.

Consider the cable show to be a low-budget, low-key version of what you get on PBS—you know, where a slide of your logo and address appears at the beginning and end of the show, and the announcer says, "This show is made possible through the generosity of XYZ Consulting Services of Maintown, USA." And if you work it right, you could probably get a blowup of your logo behind your desk or chair on camera.

Your Own Radio Show.   One of my clients, Laura Miller, a sales consultant, came to me over two years ago about putting on her own radio show. She wanted to call it "Lunch with Laura," which was the name of her monthly networking meeting.

I thought the idea great but the title off base. It would seem like a cooking show, I said, not a business consultant's show. We approached a local news-talk station that had just changed to that format and asked if we could buy a half hour of time for thirteen weeks, once a week. They were delighted, having planned to sell block segments as part of their new start-up.

We titled the show "Mastering the Business Arts with Laura Miller" (MBA, get it?). Now I had to go sell the show to local sponsors. This, by the way, is called *time brokering;* you buy a half hour block of time and resell it. The difference between your cost—in this case $250 per week, a bargain basement rate—and the amount of sponsorships sold, minus expenses, equals your profit.

Here Laura and I ran into a problem. Almost every time we tried to sell a sponsorship, the local business couldn't seem to make a decision. We got only a few sales. So what to do—abandon the show? No way. She'd put up an $800 deposit.

Laura, being the entrepreneur and sales professional she is, convinced the station to take her $800 and give her one-minute "bites" on noteworthy business tips. It worked great and started to generate good PR for her.

She then went one step further and did something even I didn't think she could pull off. She approached the station manager and made a deal—she'd train his sales people how to really sell in exchange for thirteen weeks of her own show at no cost to her. A total win-win barter arrangement.

Did it get her publicity? Well, you're reading about it as a case history in a national book on publicity, aren't you? And she gained two major corporate clients who heard about it. (She sent them her postcard flyers just to make sure.)

You can do this too, depending on your level of negotiating power. Try it.

Trade Show

Major trade shows can be a prominent source of consulting publicity, which in turn can generate business for you. To find the right show, check the *Trade Show Directory* in your local library. I'm not recommending that you run out and buy a booth, however. They are often prohibitively expensive. Most booths go for $100 per square foot, so a 10 × 10 booth is $1,000. Add to that hotel, moving, equipment, food, and other expenses, and you're looking at over $3,000 for a small show.

No, I want you to negotiate with the show promoter to be a speaker at their show. First, explain how you're a genius at generating publicity and how you'll help them with theirs. Second, show them your clip sheets and what you've generated before. If your reputation precedes you and you've made yourself a recognized expert (see Chapter 7) already, they may trade you speaking gigs in exchange for a booth. You'd win double then.

Book or Booklet, and Audiotape

One of the best ways, if not *the* best, to promote your consulting business and establish your position as an expert is to write a booklet or book or to produce an audiocassette version of your speeches, seminars, or books.

Even if you self-publish, you gain recognition and credibility when your material is credible. Once the publicity rolls out, your targets will be impressed, and rightly so, by the fact that you went to all that trouble and work to "write a book." I've self-published two and had two done by major publishing houses. There is a decided difference in the distribution and clout when you work with a publishing house, but the fact that you're in print at all gets attention.

The Easy Way to Write a Book.   Dan Poynter, author of *The Self-Publishing Manual,* talks about a unique organizing method called the *pilot system.* I'll quote from the master:

> Start by drawing up a preliminary table of contents; just divide your message into 10 or 12 chapters. Then sort all your research material and "pile it" as required. Decide on your chapter titles and . . . sort all this photo-copied material into the applicable chapter piles . . . . Add your own notes to the piles.
>
> Now spread out the individual chapters . . . . Pick an interesting pile, any one, not necessarily the first, and go through it, underlining important points and writing in your additional comments.

Then, taking one chapter at a time, put the notes in order, based on your outline, and begin to write. If you get bogged down, write what's easiest first, then go back to the other sections. Since you're going to use a computer, you can write a subhead, or section, near the end first and go back to the middle or top of a chapter later. It's doing the project in bite-sized chunks that helps you over the mental hurdle.

Now, how to write that book easily? Remember how, earlier, we talked about the list article? Since your overall article was designed with nine substantive points (the tenth being Buy Me), if you take these main points, which become your chapter titles, and do another ten-step list article for each one, you'll have 90 points. Ninety points plus a few illustrations and graphs, front matter and back matter—and voilà! your first book.

Still confused? OK, let's go back to our example of a list article, "Ten Steps to Retirement at 50." To start, we outline the general article (remember, this is just the beginning):

Step 1. Put together goals for the future.

Step 2. Check all available assets you have.

Step 3. Check all liabilities you have.

Step 4. Take each asset and study it in light of the economic, political, and social aspects of what futurists are predicting.

Step 5. Take this data, make a card for each asset, and prioritize the assets.

Now, take step 1 and explode it into "Ten Ways to Set Your Future Retirement Goals." Then take step 2 and explode it into "The Ten-Step Method for Checking Your Retirement Assets." Do this for each of the first nine steps. Each exploded article point becomes a subhead for that particular chapter. Then add a quote, anecdote, or fact to each point, and you have the guts of your book. No sweat!

Books vs. Booklets. Use the above method, but leave out most of the illustrations, examples, and so on, and you'll have a booklet. Booklets are defined as 50-plus pages. Books run at 100 pages or better.

Audiocassette Tapes. Cassette tapes can be compilations of your speeches, individual talks, or seminars, or they can feature you reading from your book outline. It's another way clients and prospects can "buy you." And with all the commuting going on, people don't have much time to read. So why not put your best material on an audio cassette and sell it.

Producing Your Cassette. Any time you give a speech, be sure to tape-record it. After you've recorded several versions of the same talk, listen to the tapes and take notes. Make sure you use a recorder that has a counter. When you come to an important point you think is worth saving, summarize it and note the counter number.

Then take your notes and the tapes to a local recording studio. They can help you put together a master tape that includes the best parts of each speech. Or you can rerecord the entire talk in-studio, using your notes as your script.

My local studio charges $45 an hour for recording and $55 an hour for editing, which is very reasonable. The duplicating house I use charges around $1.12 per finished tape, including cassette label and clear plastic case. I sell my tapes for $10 each. That's a 10 : 1 profit, friends. My books return me a 7 : 1 profit. Where else can you get such a profit margin? See why it pays to package your consulting into tapes, books, and so on?

Now send sample tapes to radio stations along with your release, and you'll book yourself on some great talk shows.

Video News Release

A video news release, or VNR, is a two-minute story on your company, professionally done, that highlights a certain story angle. A VNR is very expensive to produce, usually around $3,000 or more. While many major corporations are using them to get coverage on the network nightly news, I suggest you hold off until you're sure you want or need this type of publicity. You might, however, suggest it to some of your clients for *their* publicity. If they are major clients and hit a home run (ABC, NBC, CBS), you'll look like a hero.

The $3,000 fee should include scripting, a camera and sound crew that comes to your location, the finished two-minute segment, and satellite uplink of the VNR to at least 100 stations.

For a list of production companies that do video news releases, check your local business phone directory or Yellow Pages under "Video Production" and "Videographers."

WHICH TOOLS YOU SHOULD USE, AND WHEN

The methods you use for publicity will depend on several factors: your target audience; what they read, watch, and listen to; whether these media take certain tools (see "Setting Up Your Card File" in Chapter 5); and finally, what phase your consultancy is in. It's *start-up* if you've been at it less than two years. After that, when it's *established,* you might find yourself *switching* from one specialty to another or trying to shore up a bad *image.*

Use Table 6-1 to help you decide what methods you might want to employ. A "Yes" in the grid means you want to use that method. Ultimately, your audience and media will be the arbiters of whether you use a particular method. In certain situations, where "MUST DO" appears, you *must* use that method as part of the entire mix if you want to reach your goal.

Situation Analysis

Let's examine the four situations above by tying them in with the grid we used in Chapter 5, which takes into account what methods four newspapers take, and work out some priorities. Start by taking another look at the media analysis grid (Table 6-2). We'll rank the different publicity tools or methods in Table 6-2 by the number of papers that accept them. Our A list has the items all four newspapers accept:

- Standard press release.
- Photo with press release.
- Letter to the editor.
- Op-ed piece.
- Personnel listing.

Table 6-1. When to Use Specific Publicity Methods

PUBLICITY METHOD	CONSULTANCY PHASE			
	START-UP	ESTABLISHED	SWITCHING	IMAGE REPAIR
Tools in the Basic Press Kit				
News release	MUST DO	MUST DO	MUST DO	MUST DO
Fact sheet	MUST DO	MUST DO	MUST DO	MUST DO
Media advisory	Yes	Yes	Yes	Yes
Personal backgrounder	Yes	Yes	Yes	Yes
Photos	Yes	Yes	Yes	Yes
Clip sheet, print	Yes	Yes	Yes	Yes
Electronic contact sheet		Yes	Yes	Yes
Company history		Yes		Yes
Other Tools				
Public-service announcement		Yes		MUST DO
Op-ed piece		Yes	Yes	MUST DO
Letter to the editor	Yes	Yes	Yes	Minimal
Feature article		Yes	Yes	Yes
Featurette	Yes		Yes	Yes
Q-and-A	Yes	Yes	Yes	
News/sales letter	Yes	Yes	MUST DO	
Event	Yes	Yes	Yes	
Speech	Yes	Yes	Yes	
Seminar	Yes	Yes	Yes	
Teaching	Yes		Yes	
Radio talk show	Yes	Yes	Yes	
TV talk show		Yes	Yes	
Own cable TV show		Yes	Yes	Yes
Own radio show		Yes	Yes	
Trade show	Yes	Yes	Yes	Yes
Book, booklet	Yes	Yes	Yes	Yes
Audiotape	Yes	Yes	Yes	
Video news release		Yes	Yes	MUST DO

Table 6-2. Media Analysis Grid—Daily Newspapers (Table 5-4)

PUBLICITY TOOL	WILL NEWSPAPER ACCEPT?			
	LAT	NYT	OCR	WSJ
Standard press release	Yes	Yes	Yes	Yes
Photo with press release	Yes	Yes	Yes	Yes
Stand-alone photo	Yes	Yes	Yes	
Letter to the editor	Yes	Yes	Yes	Yes
Feature article (freelance copy)				
Op-ed piece (opinion)	Yes	Yes	Yes	Yes
Media advisory (for an event)	Yes		Yes	
New product or service release	Yes		Yes	Yes
Calendar listing—Business section	Yes	Yes	Yes	
Personnel listing (movers and shakers)	Yes	Yes	Yes	Yes
Press kit (incl. release, backgrounder, fact sheet, photo)	SIA	SIA	SIA	SIA

Key. LAT: *Los Angeles Times;* NYT: *New York Times;* OCR: *Orange County Register;*
SIA: Send if asked (send only after sending standard release, when contact person asks
for it, not before); WSJ: *The Wall Street Journal.*

Our B list has items three of the newspapers accept:

- Stand-alone photos.
- New product or service release.
- Calendar listing—Business section.

And our C list has the one item that two of the papers accept:

- Media advisory (for an event).

The next step is to put these lists together with scenarios for the four consultancy phases. But before we add the four scenarios, let's play a little with the above lists, using our common sense. In list A, we know a standard release should be sent with a photo, so that combines the first two items into one. Personnel listings are easy to do, while letters to the editor require some thinking, and a major op-ed piece requires loads of research (which is why I said no to it for start-up consultants). So let's reprioritize based on the amount of effort involved.

Revising the A list, we get:

- Standard press release with photo.
- Personnel listing.
- Letter to the editor.
- Op-ed piece.

Our B list, which includes items accepted by three out of four newspapers, is revised the same way, based on commonsense ease of work.

- Stand-alone photos.
- Calendar listing—Business section.
- New product or service release.

The C list, of course, stays the same.

Now let's take each scenario, and see if the A list changes. It will for start-up, since op-ed pieces will be eliminated—they don't have "Yes" in the Start-up column of Table 6-1.

You follow the same plan for each list.

Using All the Tools

Now that you've seen how it works, it's time to fill out your own Media Analysis Grid (Table 6-3).

First, use your media tables from Chapter 5 to determine an ABC ranking.

Table 6-3. Your Media-Analysis Grid

PUBLICITY TOOL	WILL THEY ACCEPT?			
	MEDIA 1	MEDIA 2	MEDIA 3	MEDIA 4
Publication date/day				
Subject editor/subject reporter				
Standard press release with photo				
Stand-alone photo				
Letter to the editor				
Feature article (freelance)				
Op-ed piece (opinion)				
Media advisory				
Public-service announcement				
Film				
Videotape				
Audiotape				
Freelance copy				
New product or service release				
Calendar listing				
Personnel listing				
Q-and-A				

Second, use common sense and ease of creation to rerank your A, B, and C lists.

Third, check Table 6-1 to see what you can and cannot use, depending on your situation, then cross out from your lists the tools you're not supposed to use.

Voilà—your final, prioritized list.

IMPLEMENTING YOUR FINAL LIST

Here are some final comments to help you put your list into action, whichever phase your consultancy is in.

Start-Up Consultant

If you've been in business less than two years, the situation here is to jump-start your consulting career the fastest way possible. You'll put together a basic press kit and send out the release you designed for the kit immediately. Then, follow up within one week with phone calls. When the press asks for more information, you'll happily send out the kit. Then, based on what the media take (from your media analysis grid), send each subsequent item out every two or three weeks.

Established Consultant

Even if you set up shop more than two years ago—same as above: start with the standard release. Then follow up in correct order every three weeks. At the end of each quarter, evaluate the results and start a new campaign with a fresh story angle. This means you're doing four campaigns per year, each with a different angle.

Switching Specialties

If you're known as an expert in one particular field and you have to, or want to, position yourself as an expert in another one, it's like starting over, with a slight difference—the media know you. Again, always start with the standard release, and have a basic press kit available. In this case, however, I'd follow up the release with a 750-word featurette article to show how I've become an expert in this new field. Send it three weeks after the first release.

Then follow up with others from your media analysis grid and prioritized list.

Bad Image

If you have a bad image with the media, your target audiences, or communities, I suggest you basically start from scratch. While you may have contacts, they're not happy with you. (See next chapter on how to develop relationships that work.)

There are ten methods you wouldn't use in this case—Q-and-A, sales letters, events, speeches, seminars, teaching, TV and radio talk shows, your own radio show, and audiotapes. It should be fairly easy to see why we won't use them. They're too visible and some are too sales oriented. The last thing you need right now is to make a pitch or get in exposed situations where the media can take shots at you. Better to stay low key.

Planning a Calendar

When all the above is done, it's time to plan our publicity calendar. As stated, try to send something every two or three weeks. Avoid times when your local Chamber or community is having a major event—you'll just get lost in the crowd. Also avoid major holidays, religious and ethnic dates like Cinco de Mayo, and anything else that will clutter the media's own calendar.

You're basically looking for holes where there isn't much going on (although there will never be a day when something isn't going on). But look for a period of low activity.

Looking for a Slow News Day

You want to find a day when very little news is happening. This way your story gets more of a major focus. When are they? Well, in the newspaper world, Monday is a slow news day, as is

Saturday. Since very few people read the Saturday paper, I'd opt for Monday. Send two weeks prior with a note, "You might want to use this on Monday."

And the time of the year? First quarter is always best—not much happening, it's a new year, it's fresh. Stay away from the Christmas season for obvious reasons.

SUMMARY

If after all this, you're still with me, congratulations. Take a deep breath and let's move on to the next chapter, where I'll show you how to develop a media relationship.

CHAPTER 7

Dealing with the Media

One of the key elements—if not *the* most important element—in publicity is how you deal with the media. Try to remember that, in effect, you're selling the media on your story and your consulting business. But don't act like a used-car salesman; you'll fail. Instead, do what author Jim Cathcart calls the art of "relationship selling." That is, develop long-term relationships with the media, just as you would with your clients; some guidelines on how to do this are provided later in this chapter.

MYTHS ABOUT THE PRESS

Before you begin to develop that all-important relationship, it's necessary to understand certain myths about the press—where they come from and whether or not they are true. Let me be candid with you, having been an editor and newspaper owner and having known dozens of journalists over the years. Most stories you hear about press manipulation of the news are pure fabrication, total bunk. Oh sure, there are some stories that really happened—some journalists delight in taking potshots at consultants and business owners. But for the most part (at least in print) the people I've met in the news business are ethical and professional and are just trying to do the best job they can.

So where do these myths come from? Some come from people who don't know the rules and try to push themselves on a harried journalist—like the time wasters. Time wasters? Those people targeting the wrong media with the wrong story, people who just can't take no for an answer. Then, when they can't get a story placed, they make up a myth about why they couldn't.

My friend Jan Norman of the *Orange County Register* recalls a conference we both did where she'd just finished telling a story about someone who kept calling her with a great story that, she said, "just didn't fit my column."

As we broke up into workshops, wouldn't you know: a woman who'd heard every word stopped Jan and tried to pitch her on a story. Politely Jan asked her what made her think the story would fit a small-business column? The woman made the ultimate faux pas. "Oh, I never read your column, Mrs. Norman, but I'm sure it would fit!"

Other myths, you should know, are generated by misconception. Perhaps one person has had a bad experience with a particular reporter or editor, or the general public has seen some scandal happen, and people immediately label all journalists as rotten. They then go about bashing the media to anyone who will listen, and the rumors fly.

Listen, friends: I've been there, as I've said before. Not all journalists are bad, just as all consultants aren't bad. There's a few I don't care to work with, so I don't. But I don't label *everyone* bad. And you shouldn't either.

Ten Myths

In his book *Targeted Public Relations,* author Bob Bly lists ten myths he believes to be false. Here they are, with my comments on each.

Myth 1: News Releases Don't Work Anymore.   Both of us agree, that's wrong! Bad news releases don't work and never have. They're the ones written poorly, with no clear idea of what the story is about, ill-timed and sent to the wrong person. But if you do your homework, along the lines of the lessons in Chapter 5, your news releases will generate results.

Myth 2: Legitimate Media Snub and Don't Use Publicity.   Impossible. That's how the media get 90 percent of their stories, folks. It's the old "over the transom" method, from sources they know and trust. Reporters, especially print, are now doing double and triple jobs and don't have time for the luxury of finding and researching *every* story idea. They need you as much as you need them.

Myth 3: Printed Publicity Promos Don't Work without Follow-up.   Most of the time, that's true. Remember, the key to increasing the percentages of stories the press takes from you is follow up, follow up, follow up.

However, there are times when no follow-up will get you a story, though it's rare.

Recently I did get a story on another book I've written without using any follow-up. In fact, I didn't even send a release to my local regional paper. I just happened to have the business editor on my media label list, and I sent him my current catalog of seminars and products in the mail. About three weeks later, he had a student intern call and do a story *and* photo on my home-based consultancy and the book *How to Market Your Home-Based Business.*

So how did it happen, if it's so rare? I think because I've known the business editor at the *Inland Daily Bulletin* for four years now, and I have a relationship with him. I'm one of those resident experts he calls on from time to time for quotes and information. In other words, my already developed relationship helped. But without that, a catalog or flyer to someone who didn't know me would not have gotten a story. So do it by the numbers.

Myth 4: You Need Contacts to Get Stories Printed. Bly says this is a myth, and I agree up to a point. If you don't have contacts established but use the system right, you *will* get stories. However, it helps a lot to have those contacts, those established relationships. In this case, I'd say we agree to disagree.

Myth 5: Editors Want to Be Wined and Dined. I couldn't agree more with Bob that this is a myth. Don't waste your time and energy. In six years of knowing Jan Norman, and four of knowing the *Inland Daily Bulletin* business editor, we've never broken bread together. Oh, we may in the future. But that's not what the relationship is all about.

You see, if you ask a reporter or editor to go to lunch or dinner, or have drinks, their first thought is *bribery*. And you can't get a story by bribing the press. It turns them off. The payola scandals of the '50s and '60s are still fresh in most journalist's memories. So don't.

Myth 6: To Get the Media's Attention, You Have to Be Different, Outrageous, and Creative. I tend to disagree. Different, yes; creative, yes. Outrageous as in *publicity stunt,* no. The media are looking for that special angle—not a stunt—that can relate to their readers, viewers, and listeners. The more twist the story angle has, the more likely you'll get coverage.

Myth 7: Mailing Releases Is Archaic. Use Faxes, Modems, E-mail, and Other Means. In my experience, the mail is still the best way to send a release out. But if I'm on a tight deadline and I *must* get a story or release out to the media, especially the electronic ones, I'll use a fax. I fax it after midnight, when the rates are cheaper. And it's the first thing the assignment editor or news director sees in the morning. This is especially true of radio stations with one-person news "teams"—director, reporter, editor rolled into one. These folks start their shifts at 4 A.M., and there's your release, fresh from the fax.

Myth 8: You Can't Buy Publicity with Advertising. Unfortunately, Bob's right about this one. You *can* buy a story with advertising, especially in local rural and small circulation publications. I wish that it weren't so. But with the economy as it is, with newspapers cutting staffs, losing revenue, and so on, it's become a way for them to stave off the wolves. My advice, though—DON'T! If a publication is so inept that it's forced to trade ads for editorial space, how good can the publication's reputation be? Readers see through this immediately, and it'll harm your hard-earned reputation as well. Stay away from these folks.

Myth 9: Every Fact Printed or Broadcast is Checked. As the song says, "It ain't necessarily so." The media would like you to think it is, but it's not. Most of the time journalists just don't have the time to check your releases for accuracy. That's your responsibility as a consultant. *You* must give them accurate, authoritative information and data. Sure, they'd like to check your stuff, but they're busy.

So what happens if you fudge or have info that's suspect? Will they blame themselves, those media gods? Nope, they'll blame you. And you can be sure you'll never get a story in their publication or on their station ever again.

THE GOLDEN RULE OF MEDIA: NEVER LIE TO THE PRESS. EVER. PERIOD.

A side note: To make sure you're covered, get quotes from outside sources, especially governmental, that can back up what you're saying. That way, it's not you who messed up the numbers, it's the government. For example, I once did a release on a product called the "Lotto Buster Cube," a novelty device for picking random lottery numbers. In the release, I mentioned the number of players who use the "Quik Pick," which lets a computer pick their numbers for them. I quoted a state lottery official who told me how many winners they had from Quick Picks. The sentence read: "According to Mr. XYZ of the California State Lottery, the odds against a single Quick Pick giving a winning number are 4 million to 1.

This showed a possible need for my client's product, and the quote from a state official covered my derriere. So, get an expert quote and you can't go wrong.

Myth 10: Publicity Is a Matter of Luck and Timing. Not a matter of luck, but definitely of good timing. Sending in your media materials with enough lead time, *before* deadline, and having a timely story (see Chapter 4, on story ideas) will ensure that you get more than your share of coverage.

Are the Media Out to Get You?

I don't know of many reporters or editors who are on a witch hunt per se. I do know, however, that if you lie to them, or send them inaccurate or unsubstantiated info, the next time you send something in, they'll throw it away and never cover you again.

But what about Charles Keating and the savings and loan scandal you say. Weren't the press out to get him?

Well, yes, but for two good reasons. First, he lied to people, cost them millions, and hurt and ruined their lives in the process. This is a *news* story, after all, and the press have to report it. Remember, journalists see themselves as the unsung champions of the people (rightly so), and if they uncover scandal and can help people in the process, they'll report it.

Second, Keating lied to the press in a big way. Look out . . . warpath time! No, I'm not saying that if you lie the press will go after you; you're not a major player (at least not yet). But you'll never get coverage. Keating's problem was that he lied, then tried to cover it up. A good reporter has a nose for news, and a cover-up smells like rotten meat.

Do the Media Play Favorites?

Yes, indeed. And you want to be on their hit parade. They play favorites (read "sources") with those who give them accurate, authoritative data and info they can use. Be that dependable source continually, and you'll become one of their resident experts (see below).

Look at it from their point of view. Would you rather deal with someone who regularly (1) does their homework, (2) knows what you write about, (3) is honest and aboveboard, (4) researches their stories so the article or column relates to the reader and reads well, and (5) gives you story ideas in a constant flow? Or would you rather deal with an unknown? The answer is obvious.

What If I Buy Ads and They Approach Me?

If you're a regular advertiser and are approached for a story, great—as long as they come to you and say, "We'd like to do a story on you. We see you've been advertising, and we'd like to feature what you do in an article." That's OK.

What's not OK is if they offer tit for tat—you buy an ad, we'll give you a story (most major publications *never* do this).

So, suppose you are approached about a story and you're a regular advertiser. What should you do? Just make sure *you* never bring up your advertising or how much you spend. A good reporter never will.

One word of caution: Make sure your story appears in a different section, or at least on a different page, than your regular ads. In fact if you can swing it, ask the reporter after the interview, "When do you think this might run?" Then stop your ads for those days until after the story appears. You don't want to tarnish your reputation.

APPROACHING THE MEDIA

The first time you approach the media with a news release, you're a total stranger. You must romance them. Instead of flowers, candy, candlelight, and restaurants, offer friendliness, honesty, warmth, trust, and a darned good story angle.

You must first introduce yourself. If you can, you should physically make a trip down to your local paper and introduce yourself to the reporter/editor/key contact. (Who you deal with is determined by your special area of consulting and the industries you work with.)

According to DeWitt Scott, former copy editor for the *San Francisco Chronicle,* the approach is as follows:

1. Determine the best time to visit.
2. Bring the basic material (news release) with you, but keep it under cover.
3. Don't sell the story on the first visit.
4. Follow up with a phone call about some other local story when you don't need the media. (This shows you're a good buddy.)

When's the Best Time to Contact Them?

Two schools of thought here. Many professionals say to send a release, then follow up with a phone call within three or four days *after* the target has received the material. I, and several other publicists, believe that time—both the reporter/editor's and ours—is too valuable for this approach. So I call first.

I try to leverage my time and efforts to get the most for myself and my clients. After I've targeted my media and done a prioritization (based on who I think will accept the material and how easy it'll be), I then start at the top and call my list of targets. (Of course, I already made sure of the correct name when I put my contact-card list together.) The idea—see who'd be interested in a story about such and such *before* I send the release. That way, if they're not interested, I won't waste time, postage, or money; I'll just move on to the next target on the list.

Here's a script of what I say when I make the call:

> Hello, Mr. Editor. This is Reece Franklin from Market-Smarts in Chino Hills, California. I have a story idea I'd like to run past you. Would this be a good time to talk, or are you on deadline?

Wait—didn't I say to know the deadlines in advance? True. But you never know if your contact's in the middle of a crisis story, so it's polite to ask.

They'll usually say, "What've you got?" or "What's the story about?" You then have exactly two minutes—no more, no less—to "pitch" them on the story idea.

If they're interested in the story, they'll usually ask me to mail them a release. I'll offer to fax it and get it there sooner. Either way, they're expecting it now, and when they see it, they'll be conditioned for it. That's much better than sending your release in unsolicited (they don't know about it) and having it go on the "slush" pile, that tall stack of over 200 releases per day that most newspapers and magazines get. (That's per reporter, folks, not per paper!)

After they receive the release, I wait three or four business days and then do my follow-up calls. They're much more receptive to talk features stories that way.

So there you have it. The formula again:

1. Call ahead.
2. Send the release—with photo, of course.
3. Follow up with a call three or four days later.

I'd rather have ten reporters out of a hundred show an interest in the story than send a hundred releases blindly and hope for the best.

The All-Important What Not to Say

The worst thing you can say on a follow-up call is "Did you get my release?" NEVER—repeat, NEVER—ASK IF THEY GOT THE RE-LEASE. Oftentimes I've wanted to scream at the person who asked me that, "How should *I* know? I'm buried under 300 releases from the last two days!" (I never did, but if I found their release, I usually threw it away.)

Try this instead:

"Hi, John [you've already established some rapport already, remember, since you pre-called several business days earlier]. This is Reece Franklin from MarketSmarts. I sent you that release, "Financial Consultants and the Crisis in Bosnia." Do you have any questions that weren't answered I could help you with?"

If they say, "No questions," follow with "Great. When do you think you might be able to run a story on this?" (Always be positive.)
If they have questions, answer them.

DEVELOPING THE RELATIONSHIP

There's a six-step process for beginning to develop a relationship with media people. It's a simple process that follows logic and common sense. Use it as a check-off list:

1. Target Your Media

You know how to do this from previous chapters.

2. Know What You Want to Say

Plan a two-minute pitch on your story angle. Use the five-Ws-and-H formula you've learned—the who, what, where, when, why, and how. Lead with the strongest of the elements, just as you did in your release.

3. Pick the Right Time

If you're dealing with a newspaper, know their deadlines (you find these in the media directories). If a daily paper is delivered in the morning, crunch time for reporters comes in the afternoon. If the paper has an afternoon delivery, morning is bad. When the pub hits the streets is when you should call.

If it's a weekly pub, leave them alone two days before publication date. If it's a monthly magazine, the week before going to press is deadly. Table 7-1 sums up your options for contacting the media.

Table 7-1. Best and Worst Times to Contact the Media

MEDIA TYPE	MINIMUM LEAD TIME NEEDED	TIME TO CALL BEST	WORST
Daily paper—A.M.	One week	Morning	Afternoon
Daily paper—P.M.	One week	Afternoon	Morning
Weekly paper	Two weeks	Right after deadline	Two days before deadline
Monthly magazine	Three months	One week after deadline	Two weeks before deadline
TV news	Two to four days	Morning	Afternoon
Radio news	Two to four days	Morning (9–10 A.M.)	Afternoon
Talk show	One month	Afternoon	Morning

4. Have Your Materials Already Prepared

It goes without saying; all your material should be prepared well in advance of when you make your pitch. You don't want to stutter on the phone when a reporter asks you a question. In fact, it's a good idea to anticipate the type of questions they might ask (remember the 12 Q-and-As in Chapter 6), and practice with a friend. Get the timing down for each question to about a 30-second answer.

5. Call or Visit Them

If the media is local, make that first visit, please. There's nothing better than face to face to cement a relationship. If long distance, you have to call. For more on the first visit, see "The Local Approach" below.

6. Follow Up

Never leave a possible story hanging. Always follow up with a phone call to a reporter *unless* they tell you not to.

The Local Approach

When you approach a reporter/editor, if they shoo you off, that's okay. Say that you came down to introduce yourself and meet them and that you'd like to leave your business card. If they need any information on the industries you deal with or on your specialty, you'll be glad to help. Thank them, and leave.

When you get back to the office, send a thank-you note for the time spent in meeting you. Little courtesies start you off right.

If you can't see them immediately and are rebuffed by a gatekeeper, be polite. Thank the person, take out your business card and your release, and ask that they put them on the editor's desk.

Thank them again, and leave. (You want this gatekeeper on your side.)

Back at the office, call the editor later in the day. Apologize for the inconvenience and tell them you'd stopped by to deliver some information. If they find it newsworthy, would they please schedule you for an appointment?

Key: Thank them with a note no matter what they do—story or no.

The Long-Distance Relationship

Most consultants want to hit the "big papers" so fast, they forget the impact of the local and regional press. That's why I started with the local approach in the previous section. But there are times when dealing with local papers, especially weeklies, just isn't enough.

OK, so what happens if you want to sell your story to national trade and consumer magazines or national newspapers? You can't possibly hand deliver each release around the country.

In this case, you must mail each release. However, don't send out a shotgun "blanket" release, the kind that you write once and copy hundreds of times.

Target your publications. Know what their reporters write about and how they write. Know what their favorite subjects are. This will take research, reading, and studying (see Appendix 2, "How to Study a Magazine Article"). Any consultant who wants to be able to use the media to his advantage will invest the time.

Once the release is sent, follow up with a phone call within two weeks. (Only do this for long-distance magazines and papers).

Be polite. Be brief. Get to the point. As before, don't ask if they received the release, or if they intend to use it. Assume they got it. Instead say, "Mr. Jones, this is Reece Franklin of the ABC Consultancy. I sent you a release two weeks ago regarding cleaning up the ozone layer. Do you have any questions I might answer?"

This way, you draw attention to when you sent the release, what it was about, and who you are. If they say "No questions," ask them when the story might run. If they have questions, answer them succinctly. If they can't find your release, which may happen frequently, offer to send them a new copy. Attach a cover note that says, "Here's the release we spoke about." Make sure you mention something in the letter specifically about their readership—in other words, target the cover letter. And be prepared with a local angle they can pick up.

For example, for the story about ozone layers to interest the editor, you'll have to find someone else in their area who's having problems or who is a spokesperson on the subject. This is known as the *piggyback method*—you share a story with someone else in another locality in order to gain publicity for yourself. So who cares if you're not the main feature? Take the coverage. In fact, I've done an entire campaign where I was the focal point in only five out of 30 stories. The rest featured a local inventor that I contacted with the exciting news "I'm going to get you great publicity in your local paper. I just want you to mention you've read my book or consulted with me." (Both true, by the way.) It worked like gangbusters.

BECOMING THEIR NEWS SOURCE

Once you've established a contact with the correct media person, whether locally or long-distance, you must keep the contact alive. Send them information on stories their readers might find interesting. Send them info even when you don't need them. Pretty soon, you'll find yourself becoming a source for them. That's what you want.

For example, the first time I met with Charlie Farrell, the former managing editor of the *Chino Champion,* it was for a maximum of five minutes. I'd just moved to town and had a book I wanted to pitch, my *Inventor's Marketing Handbook.*

I told Mr. Farrell I was new in town—a local author and an expert on inventors and invention marketing. He scheduled an interview for later that week. That's how easy it was.

Several months later I saw a car accident near home. The car hit a fire hydrant, and water was spurting 25 feet in the air. I immediately called the paper and told Mr. Farrell there was a great story and photo opp. (opportunity) at the corner of Pipeline and the 71 freeway. I hadn't finished my sentence before he was off the phone. Did he hang up? On the contrary, the receptionist told me he bolted out the office with his camera in hand, ready to land the "big scoop." (For a local paper, this *was* a big story.)

What did this have to do with my consultancy and inventions? Nothing. But I did him a favor. In fact, I frequently do favors for the paper. And when I want to call them with a story idea, they return my calls. Charlie and I are on a first-name basis now; we have a friendly working relationship, cemented over the years. I'm one of his sources.

Resident Expert—Your Ultimate Goal

Your ultimate challenge and goal is to become a reporter's or editor's resident expert in your industry. Whenever they need someone to answer a question about your field, or your clients', your name surfaces in their minds. You do this through various methods: relationship development, article writing, possible column assignments, and more.

After all, if Ann Landers did it, so can you. You see, Ann Landers didn't gather *all* her material by herself or through her researchers. Far from it. She had a network of resident experts, or sources, whom she called on regularly to feed her facts, quotes, and anecdotes. That's what you want—to become a resident expert to many reporters, editors, and news directors. How? By following the methods in this chapter, and by becoming an "instant expert."

Instant Expert . . . Not So Instant

To you, it won't be instant. You're going to have to take time to study your subject matter—your consulting specialty—and do several client projects using your knowledge. Once you've done this, it's time to publish that 50-page booklet we talked about in Chapter 6. Add to this a dozen speeches, and when you send your release out, you're the "instant expert."

I started teaching advertising classes and consulting part-time in 1988, and my first book was written in 1989. To the press and the outside world, I looked like an instant expert. In reality, I'd been in advertising, promotion, and fund-raising for 15 years already. I'd paid my dues.

Must you take 15 or more years to become the expert? No. Just have enough information and experience so that when you do releases on your booklet, you'll know what you're talking about and not be faking it.

The Rolodex Expert Card

One way to let the media know you're an expert on a certain subject, and available for quotes and interviews, is to have a Rolodex card made with your name, address, phone, and area(s) of expertise on it. Then send it along with your first release and photo. You'll find reporters will appreciate it and put it in their card files. See the sample Rolodex card in Figure 7-1.

WHAT TO DO WHEN THEY SAY NO

Face it. There will be times, many times, when the media say no to your story idea. Or they dump your release in the round file, you call to follow up, and they say "we junked it, it just has no life." Do you give up? And when?

Figure 7-1. Sample Rolodex card the author sends to media contacts

First, no doesn't always mean "no." It may mean "I don't have enough information yet." Without saying, "Why?" and getting the reporter all upset, I usually ask, "What was missing in the story that caused you to reject it? I'd like to know, so when I submit a future idea, it will meet with your approval." If you're polite and sincere and if you get that across, the reporter will probably tell you.

In one case, a local editor told me my story didn't have enough of a local angle (most often the case). My comment: "If I can find you two local inventors to flesh out the story, do we have something then?" He said yes, I did, we did, and the story would run with their products featured. Not to worry—I got a four-paragraph mention, after coaching the inventors on the phone for an hour about how to do an interview.

Pitch Three Times before You're Out

A fellow publicist, Devon Blaine, gave me this tip, which I'll share with you. "I train my staff," she said, "to pitch three times, from three different angles, before we give up on a particular media." I agree. Have three different angles for the story, and try all three before you give up.

Do you do this in one conversation or at three different times? Since time and patience are of the essence, try all three angles (if you need to) during the same conversation.

And if the reporter still isn't buying? Then at the very end, politely thank them, and if you feel they're receptive, say, "I understand this story isn't right for you. With your permission, is there any other reporter at your publication who's subject it would fit into better?" I've saved many a story and media outlet this way.

Comin' at 'Em from a Different Angle

In order to know, in advance, the three angles, you *must* do your homework. Read the papers you're targeting, listen to the radio shows, watch the TV shows and news. Write down three different angles of the same story, prioritize them, and go for it. For example, here are three angles on the CSEA tax story we looked at in Chapter 6.

Angle 1. How to avoid taxes at IRS time.
Angle 2. How local residents are paying more than their fair share.
Angle 3. How the IRS gets people to pay, in advance, taxes they're not liable for.

All three story angles come from the same information source. All three are really the same story. The different angles are just based on which part of the story I lead with.

How Often Should You Bug Them?

This is a tough question to answer. Some reporters don't mind phone calls on a regular basis. Some hate it. I suggest you:

- Get to know the reporter's schedule—through an initial call or a talk with the receptionist.
- Get a feel for the reporter's personality—read their articles, watch them on TV, listen on the radio, size up their voice on the phone.
- Set up a proper schedule for callbacks—not every day, but once a week unless they say otherwise.
- Don't forget—the key to publicity is FOLLOW UP, FOLLOW UP, FOLLOW UP!

The Best Way to Bug Them

Remember my story from Chapter 5 about the "nice nudge"? (Nudge—pronounced "noodge" to sound like *noodle*, not *fudge*—is a Yiddish word for a pleasant pest, one that's tolerated.) Take a second, closer look now at a nudge in action. (Figure 7-2 is the back of the contact card from Figure 5-2.) As you can see, when I was pitching Sonja Bolle of the *Los Angeles Times* for a story on my *Inventor's Handbook,* I regularly called her every three or four weeks, just to touch base, over a three-month period. During those calls, I'd politely ask how she was, what was the status of my book review and story idea, and what could I do to help.

It worked. Better than that, when she eventually assigned the book to be reviewed, she stated, "You know, Reece, normally I don't like being bugged, but you're so polite and you do it so sweetly, I don't mind your calls. You're a nice nudge."

I think that's one of the highest compliments I've ever received from an editor. Thank you, Sonja. So folks, be a nice nudge when dealing with the media.

SUMMARY

How do you develop a working media relationship? It takes hard work, patience, and time. The rules are:

- Offer them news even if it doesn't have to do with you or a client.
- Follow deadlines and protocol.
- Have a real story, not just some thrown together stuff.
- Treat them with respect and dignity, as fellow human beings—just like you want to be treated. Remember, the press doesn't owe you a story!

CHAPTER 8

Setting Up Interviews

This chapter will deal with the nuances of that all-important interview, whether local, regional, or national. We'll discuss print media, electronic media, and, specifically, talk shows. And we'll talk about your big day in the media spotlight—how to act, how to dress, and what to say.

WHO YA GONNA CALL? MEDIABUSTERS!

In order to pitch for an interview, you must obviously target the right media person. Back in Chapter 5, I gave you a grid for understanding exactly who to call (see Table 8-1 to refresh your memory).

NEWSPAPERS

The section editor or reporter may cover many beats, and the one you deal with may not be his or her priority. If you're really not

Table 8–1. Media Contacts, by Job Title (Table 5–1)

MEDIA TYPE	WHOM TO CONTACT
Newspaper—metro, daily	Section editor—sports, business, lifestyle, book review, high tech, etc.
Newspaper—weekly or local	Managing editor
Magazines	Section editor; if not sure, then contact the articles editor or features editor
Radio news	News director
Television news	Assignment editor (desk); planning desk
Radio/TV talk shows	Producers; bookers

sure who to ask for, check with the city desk or city editor and ask, "Who covers topic such-and-such?" They'll tell you.

It's a definite advantage to call the city desk in advance of talking to a section reporter. When pitching my inventor's book, I realized that at any given paper my book could be of interest to the science editor, business editor, or education editor. If I wasn't sure, even after doing my homework by reading the publication for several months, I'd call the city desk. When they referred me, I'd start the conversation with "Mr. So-and-So [the paper's city editor, his boss!] suggested I talk to you, since you deal with inventors. I have a story idea I'd like to talk to you about. Would this be something you're interested in?" This is subtle psychological warfare. His boss, who signs his paycheck, suggested you call him. Nice touch.

RADIO NEWS

Radio news directors have strange hours, and the time you have to pitch them will be very short. They normally work from about 5 A.M. to 10 A.M. Then they're gone till the next day. But since they're broadcasting between 5 A.M. and 9 A.M. (morning-drive time), I suggest you call them to pitch between 9 A.M. and 10 A.M. That's only *one hour,* folks! So make an appointment to yourself on your calendar of when to call, practice a two-minute pitch, and then do it.

TV NEWS

TV assignment editors work in a pressure cooker. Believe me, you wouldn't want to be assigned to the planning desk—it's the ultimate Maalox moment every five minutes. Fires, floods, shootings, gang-bangers. And amid all this clutter, you're trying to sell your story, which is soft news. Soft news doesn't *have* to run immediately, it can run anytime. Basically, it's filler.

Add to all this chaos the fact that TV news works in 24-hour time cycles, and you have all the elements for an impossible situation. In short, you probably won't get a story on your local news. But this can happen with the right homework. Here's how.

First, study the local 11 P.M. newscast every day for at least three to four weeks. Make a list of all local stories, and see how they rank them (what's the lead story vs. the end story?).

Second, determine how to put that human-interest element we talked about into the story.

Third, make sure your timing is perfect. Send them a release with the release date stating "For Release on MONTH DD, YYYY [an actual date]." Put a sticky note on the release: "To Planning Desk: FYI for your future file." (The *future file* is a media tickler file.)

Next, 48 hours before your event, or before the date you want the story to air, fax them another release along with a fact sheet. If you're faxing these on, say, Monday, add a fax cover sheet that says, "Available for interview Tuesday and Wednesday"—the two days *after* they receive the fax.

Finally, call up the planning desk the day before and gently ask if the story has been assigned to a reporter.

Will it work? You have a 50-50 chance at this point. To improve your chances, put together an expert's press kit (Chapter 5), call the assignment editor or desk, and tell them you're sending them a press kit with background information on your expertise. Tell them it's for them to hold, in case they ever need an expert opinion on your field. That should position you better.

TALK SHOWS

Radio and television talk shows are different animals altogether; you're never sure who you need to pitch to get on. Normally the person with the clout to get you on is called a "producer." The problem is: which producer?—executive, supervising, associate supervising, assistant supervising, line, and so on ad infinitum. The list is endless.

I once called a local talk show in Los Angeles to pitch a client. I asked for Lisa Kridos since her name had been given to me by a colleague. When the receptionist asked why, I politely told her I had a client I wanted booked on the show. She said, "Oh, Lisa doesn't do that anymore. She's now the assistant supervising line producer. [Huh? I haven't got a clue what *that* title means!] You want so-and-so."

The way to play the game—make advance calls, and ask who does the booking for guests. Get the name, the exact title (for a pitch letter), and the extension. Then, when it's time to call, you'll know who to hit.

The Radio Blitz "Hot Card"

One of my all-time favorite methods for reaching radio talk shows en masse was developed by Joe and Judy Sabah of Denver, Colorado. Joe is a master at this game and has been on over 550 radio talk shows pitching his book. His technique works with any subject, not just books. It's a concept called the *radio blitz "hot card."* Here's how it works.

First, get a list of all major radio stations in the U.S. that have talk shows. Not just any kind of talk show, mind you, but ones where you can do long-distance interviews from your office via phone. Joe Sabah sells this list, which includes over 700 radio talk shows that will interview guests by telephone, and he updates it every six months. You can also put together your own list of stations. But since Joe has already done it, why reinvent the wheel? (To contact him, write P.O. Box 101330, Denver, CO 80250, or call 303-722-7200. Ask for the Radio Talk Show System.)

Second, design a $5\frac{1}{2} \times 8\frac{1}{2}$ card that spells out exactly what you're offering the producer and host. (See Figure 8-1 for an example.) Have your typesetter lay out the card two up on an $8\frac{1}{2} \times 11$ sheet of paper, both sides. Then when you print (on card stock), you've cut your costs in half.

Third, pick a good, strong color for the card stock. This makes it stand out from all the other mail producers get. According to Joe, goldenrod is the best color. It will increase response 142 percent over any other colors.

Fourth, attach one label per card, and send them out FIRST CLASS. (No bulk mail to the media, EVER. Image, remember?)

Fifth, since you have Joe's list with the name of the contact person, you know who to call. Make those follow-up calls no later than five business days after they've received the card. And happy bookings.

One cautionary note: Be prepared for the interview instantaneously. You may find, as I have, that when you reach the producer, they're ready to put you on right away!

The first time I tried the radio blitz "hot card," I timed it to coincide with Thomas Edison's birthday. (He was an inventor, and my book was on invention marketing.) In the three weeks before and just after his birthday, I wound up with over 30 interviews.

You may not get the results Joe or I did. It depends on your subject matter, how articulate you are on the phone, and how disciplined you are about making those calls. The total investment for the initial mailing—postage, list, and cards—should be under $400.

HERE'S THE HOTTEST TOPIC FOR THESE RECESSIONARY TIMES—HOW YOUR LISTENERS CAN HAVE COMMON CENTS (SENSE) IN SAVING MONEY, AND TAKE CHARGE OF THEIR LIVES!

Available for Interviews Now!!

Publisher Cindy Landreth-Smith and Writer Laurel Dewey of

Cents & Sense
Money Saving Newsletter

Cents & Sense is the HOTTEST newsletter to come on the scene since the recession hit! Each issue is chocked full of timely advice on how to SAVE MONEY and TAKE CHARGE OF YOUR LIFE!

Publisher Cindy Landreth-Smith has been there! From near bankruptcy and unemployment to gainful employment and saving her home, she tells readers exactly <u>what to do</u> and <u>how to do it</u>!

Editor Laurel Dewey was an unemployed writer and world renowned penny pincher. She's used her expertise to turn her ideas into this dynamite newsletter!

NOW BOTH WILL TELL YOUR LISTENING AUDIENCE HOW TO <u>SAVE CENTS AND MAKE SENSE</u>

FOR BOOKING INFORMATION, CONTACT REECE FRANKLIN AT (714) 393-8525

Reece Franklin & Associates
14911 Rolling Ridge Drive
Chino Hills, CA 91709

Give your Listeners
Some Common Cents (sic) Ways
To Save Money This Fall!

Figure 8-1. Back (above) and front (below) of sample 5½ by 8½ "hot card" for radio blitz

HOW TO PITCH LIKE A WINNER

The pitch letter and the pitch phone call are at the core of whether or not you land an interview. In Chapter 7 we discussed the pitch you use for print media. If you're unsure of what to say, review that chapter first.

For television, the pitch is made with a TV media kit followed up by a phone call. For radio, the "hot card" method works great.

Pitching for Television

A media kit is the first step in getting yourself booked on television. It should be unique and exciting, not just a plain-vanilla type. Remember, television is a visual medium, so what you send for print won't necessarily work for TV (although several of the elements do overlap).

According to Wicke Chambers and Spring Asher, authors of *TV PR* (Rocklin, Ca.: Prima, 1987), you should include the following in your TV media kit:

- A cover letter.
- A biography of the guest (you).
- The fact sheet.
- Background information.
- Suggested questions.
- Print media clippings.
- A photo or horizontal slide.
- Visuals (pictures, slides, props, video tapes).
- The product, if it's something compact (like a book), or a picture of the product, if it's something too large to carry in one hand (optional).
- An electronic contact sheet.

What should you have in the cover or pitch letter for a TV talk show? Enough to get the producer or assignment editor excited about the proposed interview. It should be one page in length, with four short paragraphs. Figure 8-2 gives you an example.

Notice the format of the letter. It leads with a shocker—"Inventors create some of the weirdest gizmos, yet the things actually work!"

Paragraph 2 gives some brief biographical data on you. Paragraphs 3, 4, and 5, the heart of the letter, furnish intriguing details about what you have to share (a "Preg-a-phone," a "Body Butter Batterer"), send home the message that you're more than a talking head (you'd bring "an array of . . . visually weird products"), and

---

[sample pitch letter for TV]

March 1, 1991

Ms. Pat Ellwood
Producer
"Sun Up, San Diego"
KFMB-TV
7677 Engineer Rd.
San Diego, CA 92111

Dear Pat,

"Inventors create some of the weirdest gizmos, yet the things actually work!" This according to Reece Franklin, author of *Inventor's Marketing Handbook,* AAJA, 1989. He should know.

Franklin has worked with inventors since 1986. With over 3,000 copies sold to individual inventors alone, Franklin gets more than his share of strange requests to help market these "offbeat" products.

Products like the Preg-a-phone, to help moms-to-be talk to their unborn babies in the womb. The Puffer Snuffer, for dousing a cigarette or cigar. The Body Butter Batterer, for basting yourself with tanning lotion. And many others.

Franklin's contacts with inventors' clubs, trade shows, and the industry have helped him round up this array of unusual and visually weird products that your viewers will find fascinating.

Most of the products, once described, elicit an "of course, that's what it is!" But sitting on a table, no one knows. This makes for great audience participation.

Franklin plans on visiting the San Diego area between April 15 and 17 to help celebrate the anniversary of Ben Franklin's passing. In keeping with the auspicious occasion, he can dress in colonial garb and give your viewers a succinct history of the great inventor. We can furnish slides of other successful inventions as well.

Figure 8-2. Sample pitch letter for TV

then tell why viewers will be enthralled ("great audience participation").

The final paragraph tells when you'll be available for interviews and, to strengthen the close, gives one or more secondary reasons why you'd make a terrific guest.

The Phone Pitch. Your phone pitch should follow the arrival of the media kit by no more than three business days. For a good opener, tell them your name, that you sent them a media kit, and something that ties into the kit and your expertise. For example:

> Hi, Ms. Ellwood. This is Reece Franklin. I sent you a kit on the "strange inventions" segment—the Puffer Snuffer and the Preg-a-phone. You know, over 50 percent of the people in San Diego are wanna-be inventors. I think there's a local story here you might want to do about your area inventors and their unique products.

Open your pitch with an attention-getter. Remember, this is a sales presentation. In fact, you might want to use the sales formula called A-I-D-A—attention, interest, desire, action. Start your pitch with the attention step; create interest by showing how your topic relates to their audience; turn interest into desire by describing the great visuals; then ask for the order—"What data can you see us doing the segment on your show?" (Again, positive assumptions work.)

If the pitch is for radio, there are no visuals. Still, mention that you've been on other radio or TV shows so they know you're not a rookie. Tell the radio producer how you can make the show "come alive" by describing your best story or anecdote about a client.

If this is your first media interview, it'll show. Everyone has to start out somewhere, however. I suggest you try a local cable talk show to get your feet wet. Make a video copy of your interview, and study what you did right and wrong.

THE THREE-WAY PITCH—THREE STRIKES IS NOT OUT

As stated in the last chapter, it's important to pitch three times before giving up. So have three angles in mind when you pitch TV and radio personnel. For the above story on inventions, I had the main angle, weird inventions, and two backups, local inventors and a local engineering school that was creating a faster engine part. Fortunately, I only needed the main angle because I could pitch its strong visual appeal. (Use Figure 8-3 to select three story angles and three pitches that can work for you.)

Why do I say three strikes is not (necessarily) out? Simple. You've only tried pitching on *one* story idea, not on all of them. Start over. You may hit a producer's hot button later in the month, or year. Also, producers change regularly—especially on local shows. The one who said no today may not be there next month. So do your homework to see if the first producer is gone, then pitch the same story from a slightly different angle, and chances are they'll say yes. Congratulations!

STORY ANGLE	SCRIPT FOR PITCHING THIS ANGLE
1.	
2.	
3.	

Figure 8-3. Three-angle worksheet

165

LANDING THE INTERVIEW

Once you land an interview, the work's just begun. Make sure you send a confirming letter to the producer, using the who, what, where, when, and why formula. Creating the media kit and this letter helps you focus your thoughts on exactly what you intend to say during the interview.

SCHEDULING

Since you're going to be working on multiple media, both print and broadcast, it's essential to have a calendar for scheduling what to do and when your interviews are. It makes no difference what kind of calendar you use. Just be sure to mark interview dates in red and to use a different color for the dates you sent out material.

If you intend to do a publicity tour, be sure to leave enough room during the week for several interviews. Don't crowd your day with one appearance after the other. Missed flights, missed taxis, and interviews that run long are all common. Leave at least 1½ hours between interviews for travel. See Figure 8-4 for a guide.

GETTING READY FOR INTERVIEWS

What should you do to look good during an interview? Suffice it to say, you'd better be prepared. And to be well prepared, there are several steps you need to take.

First, from a list of a dozen questions they could ask, pick the top three you think they'll ask. Hopefully, the priority is fairly obvious, so that you pick 1-2-3 and they ask 1-2-3—but you never know. Memorize the answers. Then go to the next three and the next until you have good answers for all twelve.

JUNE 1996

SUNDAY	MONDAY	TUESDAY	WEDNESDAY	THURSDAY	FRIDAY	SATURDAY
26	27	28	29	30	31	1
	Final pitch to L.A. TV Stations			Fax Schedule to Natl. Stations		
2 Fly to Chicago, American Airlines #768 at 3 P.M.	3	4 8:00 WBBM Radio - Interview from home office	5 1:30 WGN Radio	6 8:30 WMAQ Radio	7	8 Fly to LA, AA #287 at 1 P.M. 6:00 Holiday Inn, A/P
	Fax Schedule Local Media		Final Confirmation Calls			
9	10	11 National Inventor's Day Promotion 7:00 Today Show 8:00 GMA Nat'l 9:00 KABC Local	12 11:00 LA Times 1:00 Valley News 3:00 KIEV Glendale Radio	13 8:00 OC News 9:30 Orange County Register 1:00 CNBC	14	15 Fly Home, AA #568 at 5 P.M.
16	17	18	19	20	21	22
		Revise Clip Sheets				
23	24	25	26	27	28	29
	Send Thank-you Letters to All Media					

Figure 8-4. Sample calendar showing how the author schedules a publicity tour (circled entries would be written in red ink)

167

Second, cut your answers down to 30 seconds or less. This means scripting, editing, and rehearsing them until they're perfect. Thirty seconds is roughly the timing for what the industry calls a *sound bite.*

Third, to make sure this sound bite is positive, work with a friend or speech coach until it's reworded and reordered so that no matter what the interviewer asks, the answer is positive to your consultancy.

Fourth and finally, pick three bits of information you want to leave with the audience. These should be the top three points you want to make. Practice with your coach how you'll work them in if the interviewer doesn't ask them. For example:

> INTERVIEWER: Reece, I see that you've brought some really weird gadgets. But none of them made any money, did they?
>
> ME: On the contrary, Gary, several did quite well. For instance, the anti-smoking mask. And that's what I teach in my inventor's seminar coming up this week at SDSU—how to turn a mediocre product into a winner. [Here I've brought in the last of my three points, a seminar I was holding that weekend.]
>
> INTERVIEWER: Come on, Reece, do you really expect people to make millions from their products?
>
> ME: The money is secondary, Gary. Most people invent to solve their own particular problems and make their life easier. If they happen to make money along the way, that's gravy. [My second point—why people invent.]
>
> INTERVIEWER: All right, I'll buy that. Now just how do people come up with ideas? [At last, one of my actual questions!]

168

ME: I'm glad you asked, Gary. You see, anyone can invent something. Just by strolling down a shopping aisle, they'll see something that triggers "I can make that better" or "If only they'd invent a whatsit for whatever." And that's when the creative juices start to flow.

Three Top Answers That Can Position You as an Expert

In preparing for a media interview, it's important to have in mind the top three answers you want to leave with the radio or TV audience. What these keys to your expertise are depends on your field and, specifically, on which nuggets of information are startling facts that most of your audience don't know already.

Unfortunately, I can't say what *your* top three are—you have to figure this one out for yourself. But it should be easy. Start by searching your knowledge database and writing down several tips you think people don't know. Then call a dozen friends and clients, tell them you're researching for a radio or television appearance, and ask, "If you heard this on a talk show, would it be new information to you, or old hat?"

Another way to find out which of those nuggets are unknown is to do several college workshops. Offer your best material, and take a survey at the end to see what people knew and didn't know. The simple grid of Figure 8-5 gives you a structure to help you make choosing three top nuggets part of your normal preparation for an interview.

Working with Producers

You must develop relationships both with the print media and with television and radio talk-show producers. You do this by following their rules, meeting deadlines, offering exciting visuals and info for their audiences, and never lying.

NO.	ITEM OF INFORMATION
1.	
2.	
3.	

Figure 8-5.   Information that my audience may not know—worksheet

Once you develop that relationship, solidify it by offering, in a short note, suggestions for other segments, even if these have nothing to do with your expertise. (Note the similarity to print media.) Say you just happened to hear or see such and such, and you thought it would make a good segment. Don't do this every week or month but only when you truly have a gem. You'll become a source and be the guest with "the nose for news."

What If You Get Blindsided?

It happens to the best of us. We've done our homework, practiced our questions and answers, role played, even taken a coaching lesson or two. We appear at the studio, get warm assurances everything is fine, and then the interviewer, who may or may not have consulted with the producer, blindsides us. Wham! A question out of left field we're not prepared for. What can you do?

To start with, keep your composure. Some interviewers just love to rattle our cages. Keep cool, smile warmly, look them in the eye, and say, "That's a point I'm sure we can cover in another interview. In the meantime, it's important to realize that . . . ." You put the interview back on course this way.

Second, prepare in advance. Try to think of *every* possible question they could ask, so you're not left holding dead air.

Third, don't ever argue, on camera or off.

Finally, if you don't know the answer to a question, be honest. Say "That's a good question, but I don't know the answer. However, I can find out for you for another interview."

This happened to me several years ago. A client was prepped for an interview. The assignment editor assured me the interviewers would stick with the prepared questions. (I should have known better the minute she mentioned it for the third time.) My client got on camera, all nervous and sweating (also my fault—we should have rehearsed longer) and SMACK! A question on his credentials. He was so rattled, he paused for a full ten seconds. Dead air = bad impression. We were not asked back. By the way, he *had* the credentials, but neither of us assumed they'd be suspect. The interviewer, fortunately, has gone on to greater shark glory in some small rural town, reading the weather.

Types of Interviewers

In his book *How to Get Publicity* (Times Books, 1985), William Parkhurst offers a list of seven terror interviews and how to handle them. They range from the "Ken and Barbie" show to the interrupter. Table 8-2 summarizes how to solve them.

The Big Day

So it's here at last, your big day to shine under the studio lights or in the radio studio. Relax. You'll do fine. Just a few more points to remember.

How to Keep Control.   You know what to say; you've practiced over and over. Don't take your written script with you—you

Table 8-2. Strategies for Handling Difficult Interviewers

INTERVIEWER TYPE	HOW TO HANDLE
Ken and Barbie (vapid beauties)	Give them respect in a non-patronizing way. Bring conversation around to your topic with "I've developed another area of expertise in . . . ."
Mini-Mike (thinks he or she is Mike Wallace)	Be calm. "I'm glad you asked that. As you know, [insert statistic] . . . ."
Terrorist	Excuse yourself and leave studio.
Dr. Sensitive (wants to psychoanalyze you on the air)	Gently: "I don't think a public forum is the best place for me to discuss this."
Catatonic (brain on hold)	Pause a moment, ask them a question that relates to a key point. They'll recover when you ask them.
The Pal (watch out— could be lulling you to sleep)	No such thing as "off the record." Everything you say is fair game. Bring your own recorder to tape interview.
Interrupter	Stick to your material, in bite-sized chunks. Respond briefly to each new question, then go back to material.

might tend to read it verbatim. Instead, take one or two note cards with the three key points written down. Whenever you feel the interview slipping away from you, quickly glance at the notes. Then get back on track.

How to Dress.   What should you wear? You're a professional consultant. So dress for business. Men, it's suits and ties if you're in a major metro area, like New York or Los Angeles; coats, slacks, and ties if elsewhere. Women, wear what you'd normally wear to give a speech. If in doubt, study the interviewer on camera for several days before your appearance, and mirror the style they wear (unless they're totally flamboyant or the Ken and Barbie type).

As to colors, DON'T WEAR WHITE. It glares on camera. Wear soft blue or light pastels. No loud patterns or plaids. For men, watch the president when he's doing a press conference; you couldn't do better. Women, take a tip from Barbara Walters, always a class act.

My best advice—hire an image consultant for two hours; trade services, your consulting for hers. Let her go through your closet and rip it apart. That's what mine did. It hurt, but I looked great on camera.

How to Act. LIKE THE PROFESSIONAL THAT YOU ARE. PERIOD.

Running through the Final Act

Just before you go on, take a deep breath, check yourself in the mirror, smile big, and think of the most pleasant experience in your life. Then walk on stage with confidence that you can do the job. I know you can do it. I'll see you on TV!

CHAPTER 9

Emergency Principles

It's very possible that you may do everything right—dot every *i* and cross every *t*—and still wind up with negative publicity. Your professional associations may have a bad image in the minds of the media, and you're linked to them. Or your industry may have a sudden crisis, and you find yourself being fired on from all sides to explain why "you consultants are doing such-and-such to so-and-so."

While we can't stop negative publicity from happening entirely, we can control how we react to it.

First and foremost, *don't react;* be proactive. By planning in advance for something negative that could happen, by designing a well-thought-out method of dealing with crises, you take a positive approach. In other words, you don't shoot from the hip. As the Boy Scout motto says, Be Prepared! We ARE Prepared!

WHAT TO DO BEFORE THE RELEASE HITS THE FAN

The first step in preparing for damage control is to avoid being caught off guard by the media. Know exactly what your release said, verbatim. Memorize it. Not so that you can regurgitate it to a reporter but so you have the facts *exactly* as they were stated. You don't want to be thumbing through copy to find out "what exactly did I say?"

Step two: BEFORE you send out *any* media materials, look them over carefully. Underline any possible areas where there are inconsistencies, any places that might be subject to more than one interpretation. Then show them to your spouse, several friends, or clients you trust, and ask for their input. (You might ask them if you can use them as a case history, thus solidifying your relationship.)

Wherever they think you mean one thing when you actually mean another, rewrite.

Step three: I'd take one more cautious approach before sending out material. Try to find a local college professor of journalism, and ask for their input. Tell them you want to make sure *your* interpretation of the release or article will be the same as that of the journalists you're sending the material to. Professors love this side work ($15 to cover their time is the max I've paid), and they love the flattery.

The You're-Just-Another-Consultant Syndrome

The problem with consulting is there's no credentialing or certification for most of our subspecialties. Or for consultants in general. Anyone can hang up a shingle and call themselves a consultant. As you'll see in the Appendix interview I had with Jan Norman of the *Orange County Register,* she believes the negative connotations of *consultant* are diminishing (at least for business reporters).

But since we still have a stigma attached to our profession, do all that you can to prepare in advance to overcome any negatives BE-FORE you send out release one. Here are a few suggestions.

Join the association of consultants that's closest to your specialty or subspecialty. In my case, I'm a member of the American Marketing Association, and the Book Publicists of Southern California. (By the way, this looks great on your letterhead—it shows you're a dues payer.)

Get involved early in at least one community group, and provide a pro bono service in exchange for membership. Your community standing will improve, and you'll gain valuable allies and publicity.

Pick one of the associations you've joined, and position yourself by becoming an officer. Start with the publicity role, using the techniques you've learned in this book. As you hone your skills, you'll find you're generating publicity not only for your group but for yourself as well. It's a great practice forum for you.

Pick one charity, and tie yourself into their publicity mill. Even if you only volunteer one day per quarter to help them out, it's more than your competitors do. It shows you care.

Now that you've seen my suggestions, you may be questioning my wisdom. After all, there's all this volunteerism and no paid gigs, as they say. When will you do your own publicity, run your consulting business, and deal with clients?

Folks, this is called *networking.* You'll probably get clients out of the close ties you make. And you'll make friends who will stand by you if you have that emergency situation. I'm not telling you to take up all your time. Just one or two days per quarter per group. With four groups, that's eight days out of 90—not too bad.

Preparing in Advance for Damage Control

As I said, the time may come when you are under fire. To prepare in advance for damage control, brainstorm with other consultants you know and friends—what are the two or three worst possible scenarios I may be caught up in? For example, take your best two clients, and analyze everything that could possibly go wrong.

Then put together a special *emergency* media kit, to be used only in case of damage control. It should include:

- Client histories, showing your relationship with them and what you've done for them over the past year.
- Case histories of other clients, showing positive work done.
- Your standard company history, emphasizing all the positive.
- Your biography.
- A fact sheet.
- Print media clippings.
- Testimonial letters from satisfied clients.

Making Yourself Media-Ready

The absolutely BEST way to prepare for a crisis beforehand is to practice as if it already happened. In his article *"Shining in the Spotlight"* in (*Leadership* annual, 1993), Don Skiados cites seven steps that will help.

First, develop your message. Focus on the message you want to deliver. Create file cards to outline it, then phrase it into 20-second sound bites. Have an alternate message to fall back on if you get sidetracked.

Second, have an objective. Have a goal in mind—like those three tips you want to leave with your audience, which we talked about in Chapter 8.

Third, use anecdotes and analogies. Dry facts don't work in emergencies. Create a visual palette of stories—let your words paint pictures. For example, "We've been able to save over 4,000 hours of man-time consulting to ABC Company" is not as effective as "We've saved ABC Company enough hours to give everyone in this community an extra two days vacation."

Fourth, anticipate the questions. Expect hard, biting questions—
*How could you let this happen? Aren't you afraid of the fallout?
Why weren't you concerned in advance? What are you going to
do to solve the problem?* You must take control of the interview.

Fifth, Practice, Practice, Practice. No explanation needed here.

Sixth, wear conservative clothing. Dark, plain, presidential looking.

And seventh, know the rules. Know in advance what the rules normally are, even though in a crisis situation, rules sometimes go out the window, along with normal. So be prepared to play by the rules, but also expect the unexpected. And when it comes, instead of saying "No comment," answer truthfully and as honestly as you can.

A few more *don'ts* from Don:

- Don't restate an opposing point in your answer.
- Don't be defensive.
- Don't be stunned into silence. If it's an outrageous statement, say so and return to your message.
- If interrupted, return to what you were saying. Use "as I was saying" or "the point I was making was".
- Don't use a terse yes or no.

HOW A CRISIS CAN HELP YOU

Most of the time, consultants have few problems with emergency publicity crises; it's the clients that have the problems. By teaching this chapter's methods to your clients, you can become an expert they have to have around. You'll be their hero.

Of course, you'll want to be their hero in good times as well as bad. To do that you have to be able to show your clients how you've made a difference. So in our last chapter, we'll take a look at how to measure the results of our publicity campaigns, using specific media forms and charts.

CHAPTER 10

Measuring Results

While most advertising and marketing programs have built-in and regularly established tracking methods, publicity has very few. I'm not sure if it's because the results are intangible, or what.

You see, how do you measure a story printed about you? By the calls you get that convert to clients? By the number of books you sell off a TV interview? And if there are no direct calls or sales, was the publicity a failure, even if 50 million people saw your story on the nightly news?

INTANGIBLE VS. TANGIBLE RESULTS

Intangible results are those that arise from indirect means. You send out a release, the story runs, you copy it on your letterhead, and send it to your clients and a prospect list. Off that one direct mail you get several inquiries, which lead to new clients. And you solidify your relationship with current clients. That's indirect and intangible. You can't really put a dollar-and-cents value on it until well down the road, if at all. But it does build your credibility.

The reason it works is the third party endorsement which media hits show. Now it's not just you saying you're great, it's the esteemed fourth estate, the public press saying you're great.

Tangible results would be any direct clients or sales that can be attributed directly to a story. When the prospect says "I saw you on *Oprah,* and I want to buy your book" that's a direct and tangible result.

RETURN ON INVESTMENT

According to several marketing specialists I know, Return on Investment Ratio, or ROI, is the *only* accurate way to measure results. The formula is this:

Total dollars generated by a promotion ÷ total cost of the promotion.

For example, if your publicity release with writing, postage, printing, and follow-up calls costs $2,000 and if you generate enough business or product sales to match that $2,000, your ROI is 1:1. In other words, break-even.

While break-even isn't great, it's not bad either. At least you haven't lost.

Yet since we don't know what the intangible results will be over the year or two following a story, we really can't say. The ROI might be better than break-even.

Timing also makes the ROI formula invalid for publicity. You see, ROI is calculated for a fixed and manageable time period. It has to be, to be useful. But the residual effect of publicity can last as long as people's memories—far beyond the time period you're measuring.

Bottom line—I just don't use or recommend ROI for publicity measurement.

THE ONLY RELIABLE WAY TO MEASURE

Most publicists agree—the way to measure the bang you've gotten for your publicity buck is to translate your print or broadcast hits into dollars. For example, what would it have cost you in space (print) or time (broadcast) if you'd had to pay for the same exposure? The larger the story or longer the interview, the higher the dollar results.

Recently I had a story on my new book in the *Inland Daily Bulletin*. It ran two columns wide and about ten inches high, without picture. (The picture added another eight inches or so.) Based on the *Bulletin*'s rate card, a 20-inch display and would've cost me approximately $640.00. That's $32 per inch times 20 column inches. (A column inch is one column wide by one inch high.)

So that's what I'll put on my tracking sheet (see Table 10-1).

Now it's your turn again. Figure 10-1 is for you. Use one worksheet for print media and another for electronic. List in the first column every media where you sent material. Under "To Whom" put the position of the person you sent to at that media; your contact cards (Chapter 5) should help.

Under "Date Used" put "None" if the media didn't use your piece. How do you know they haven't run it? With print media,

Table 10-1. Print Media Tracking Sheet for "Home-Based Business Increases in Inland Empire"

Media	Date Sent	To Whom	Date Used	Inches or Time
Inland Daily Bull.	4/11/95	Bus. Ed.	4/19/95	20 col. in.
S.B. Sun	4/11/95	Mg. Ed.	None	————
Riverside Press	4/12/95	Bus. Ed.	5/6/95	4 col. in.
Chino Champion	4/12/95	Mg. Ed.	5/11/95	15-1/4 col. in.

MEDIA	DATE SENT	TO WHOM	DATE USED	INCHES OR TIME

Figure 10-1. General media tracking sheet

buy the publications for three weeks or subscribe to a clipping service and have them look for and send any articles to you. If you don't get a story within three weeks from the time the media received your material, they won't be using it. For electronic media, the reporters will tell you when you're going to air. If you don't hear from them within two weeks, better luck next time.

When your story appears in print, count the column inches the way I do in Table 10-1. If you've got a possible piece running on the air, be sure to tape all newscasts. When you time the segment later with a stopwatch, include the anchor's lead-in. These numbers will be the basis for an objective record that backs up the dollar value you claim for your publicity.

OK, you've tabulated the results of your campaign in Figure 10-1. To finish the job, use Figure 10-2 to make a worksheet like Table 10-2 (based on the data in Table 10-1). List again the name of any media where you got a hit and the actual number of column inches (print) or amount of airtime (electronic) your story received there. Then list the *billing* inches or airtime. For print media, round up anything that's not an exact multiple of inches—that's how the billing departments typically count it (for example, count 3 ½ inches as 4). For electronic media, count the airtime as multiples (for

Media	Actual Inches or Time	Billing Inches or Time	Media Rate	Value of Coverage
Total				

Figure 10-2. Worksheet for calculating the value of publicity

Table 10-2. Value of Print Publicity for "Home-Based Business Increases in Inland Empire"

MEDIA	ACTUAL INCHES OR TIME	BILLING INCHES OR TIME	MEDIA RATE	VALUE OF COVERAGE
Inland Daily Bulletin	20 in.	20 in.	$32/in.	$640
S.B. Sun	——	——	——	——
Riverside Press	4 in.	4 in.	$35/in.	$140
Chino Champion	15-1/4 in.	16 in.	$22/in.	$352
Total	39-1/4 in.	40 in.	——	$1,132

example, count 50 seconds as two 30-second spots and three minutes as three 60-second spots).

Next, enter what the media's applicable rate would be if you were buying advertising. If you're tracking print media, just put down their 1 × open column inch rate. If you're tracking broadcast media, put down how much they charge for the spot length you used to calculate the billing time (30 seconds, 60 seconds, etc.).

Where do you get these rates? For local media or major out-of-town print media, the advertising departments will be happy to send you their rate list. If you get lucky and out-of-town electronics pick up your story, you can get figures from *Brook's Standard Rate Book* or the *Standard Rate and Data* series of books (see Appendix 7). Be careful, though—the published rates may be out of date.

Now for the fun. Multiply the number of inches or multiples of spot time by the appropriate rate and that's your value for the coverage. Enter it in the last column total to get the full tangible value of your campaign.

One More Grid for the Road

I know, I've gridded you to death in this book. Sorry, but I'm a visual person, and I assume you are, too. It makes it easier to read.

For all of that, let's take one last look, in Table 10-2, at our campaign media tools and what they've achieved for us in terms of hard dollars. As you can see, the result was $1,132 worth of publicity for four releases, envelopes, and 32-cent stamps. Not bad!

THE WINNER—AND STILL CHAMPION

Congratulations! You've done it. You actually finished this book and have some idea—hopefully, a pretty clear idea—of what this publicity game is all about.

As with any new skills, it takes practice to develop them and hone them to a sophisticated level. But you can do it; you're a pro. Let me give you one last piece of advice on how to polish your exciting new skills.

Go back and reread this book chapter by chapter; and do the exercises s–l–o–w–l–y. Make sure you use your clients' and business specialties as the input for the personality profile, story ideas, formulas, tracking sheets, and the like.

Then, when you've mastered a chapter, go over it with a friend or partner and discuss what can be improved. But don't do too many rewrites. After all, you want your material fresh, not worked into two dozen versions that are sick from paralysis by analysis. (Three or four rewrites should be the max.)

Then send out your material the way you've learned, and voilà. I'll see your name in print and in lights. Good luck!

A PERSONAL NOTE

I always like to end my books on a positive note, and I believe in giving you more than you paid for (added value). So here's my offer to you.

MEASURING RESULTS

After reading this book, or a particular chapter, if you're still stuck, write or call me at:

MarketSmarts
14911 Rolling Ridge Drive
Chino Hills, CA 91709
(909) 393-8525

I'll give you a FREE 15-minute critique of your release or story idea (one per consulting company). That's a $50 value, folks, based on my hourly rate. It more than pays for this book you bought! And it keeps me in touch with you, my readers.

Best regards.

Reece Franklin

How to Prepare and Market Articles that Sell (or Sell Your Consulting Services)

Gordon Burgett
(Adapted for Consulting by Reece Franklin)

1. In one sentence, what is the subject of the article you want to write about that will sell your consulting services?

2. Who would benefit (potential clients) from reading your article? Who would be most interested? What kinds of readers (clients) would select your specific subject from a variety of choices? Rank all of those potential readers (clients) in order, placing those who would derive the most benefits first.

3. Which publications do these readers (clients) buy and read? Prepare a market list of those publications that are the most likely to take your article.

4. In addition to the publications checked in (3), it is necessary to review the broader publishing field for articles similar or identical to yours. Therefore, you must check InfoTrac Computer Database for articles run in the last three years similar to yours. Then:

- List the articles that are closest to your subject, in order, with the most similar first: subject, author, title, publication, page reference, length, and when they appeared. Where the subjects appear to be very similar, how does yours differ?
- Cross-check newspaper databases for the past three years, and provide the same information.

5. Have the publications listed in (3) and (4) printed articles within the past three years that are similar to the one you want to write? If so, change the angle or come up with a different story altogether.

6. After each publication, note the name of the person you should contact (editor, managing editor, reporter, etc.) with title and address. Then provide the following information about each publication:
   - Does it prefer query or a direct submission?
   - How often is it published?
   - What percentage is written by freelancers? (The more it accepts freelancers, the more you can be sure it will take your publicity piece.)
   - What is the preferred manuscript length?
   - Any other information that will affect its ranking

7. Now rank your market list in priority order, based on frequency of publication, and the percentage of freelance material used per issue as primary criteria.

8. Read the latest issues of your target publication, front to back. Select the articles that are the most similar, in form if not topic, to the piece you will prepare. Outline each article. Write out the lead and conclusion of each, by hand. Follow the 12 steps in "How to Study a Printed Magazine Article" (Appendix 2). Attempt to identify the publication's readers by age, sex, occupation, income range, education, residence, and other important factors.

9. To verify the availability of resource information:
    - Read as many of the articles in (5) as necessary or possible, then list the sources of information found in each.
    - Consult the computer database of the library's collection, and list books to which you'll refer for factual information: title, author, call number, date of publication, and library.
    - List the human resources you should consult for additional info and quotes.

10. From the researched and specific target publication information gathered, select the material needed to write a professional query letter. Verify its accuracy.

11. Write a selling query letter to an editor of your target pub. If you don't receive a positive reply, go to the next on your list, and so on, one editor at a time, until an editor does say yes. Repeat as much of (9) as necessary for each new publication queried.

12. When you receive that positive reply to your query, plan your article to determine what is still needed for its completion.

13. Complete the needed research.

14. Write the article in final draft form. Include, on separate paper, at least five additional, different leads.

15. Select the best lead, edit the draft, type a final manuscript (keeping a copy), and mail it, with illustrations (if needed) to the editor.

APPENDIX 2

How to Study a Magazine Article

Gordon Burgett

1. Read the article closely, then ask yourself what basic or working question it answers. Write the question out. It may also answer secondary questions, so write those out too.

2. Now read the write-up for that publication in the *Writer's Market* for the year of (or preceding) the article's appearance. Given the working question in (1) and the indications in the *Writer's Market* of what that magazine was seeking, try to put yourself in the writer's shoes. How did the writer slant the subject to appeal to the magazine's readers? Why did the editor buy it? Study its length, illustrations, position in the mag.

3. To see how the writer carries the main theme through the article, underline each word that relates directly to that theme, then outline the entire piece. Study the writer's use of facts, quotes, and anecdotes. What is the ratio between them? How is humor used? Is it spread and bal-

anced to the same degree throughout? Do other articles in this issue use facts, quotes and anecdotes, and humor in roughly the same way and in the same proportion?

4. List every source used, including direct references and quotations. Where would the writer find the facts, opinions, and quotes that are not clearly identified by source in the article? If you are uncertain, indicate where you might find the material—or where you would go to find out.

5. Focus on the quotations. Why is each used? How does it carry the theme forward? Note how the source of the quotation is introduced and how much the reader must know about the source to place the person and what is said into perspective.

6. Is the article written in first person (I), second (you), or third (he, she, or it)? How does that strengthen the article? Does the person change? Why or why not? Are most other articles in the same issue written in the same person?

7. Set the title aside and concentrate on the lead. How long is it, in words or sentences? How does it grab your interest? Does it make you want to read more? Why? How does it compare with other leads in that issue?

8. Most articles begin with a short lead followed by a longer second or third paragraph that ties the lead to the body of the article. Called the transitional paragraph, it tells where you are going and how you will get there. It bridges the attention-grabbing elements of the lead to the expository elements of the body by setting direction, tone, and pace. Find the transitional paragraph and study it. Organizationally, after the lead it is the most important item in the article.

9. Now underline the first sentence in each graph. They should provide a rough chain that will pull you through

the piece. Note how the writer draws the graphs together with transitional words and phrases. Circle the words that perform this linking function. Often the same words or ideas will be repeated in the last sentence of one graph and the first sentence of the next.

10. Earlier, you outlined the article. Now look at the transitional words and the underlined first sentences and see how the structure ties the theme together. Is the article structured chronologically, developmentally, by alternating examples, point by point? Or if the article was written to answer the working question you isolated in (1), did the answers to the secondary questions stemming from that working question provide the article's organizational structure?

11. How does the article end? Does it tie back to the lead? Does it repeat an opening phrase or idea? The conclusion should reinforce and strengthen the direction the article has taken. Does it? How?

12. Finally, look at the title. It may have been changed or rewritten by the editor. Nonetheless, does it correctly describe the article that follows? Does it tease, quote, pique one's curiosity, state facts? What technique does it use to make the reader want to read the article?

APPENDIX 3

Query Letters

A query letter is used to pique the interest of an editor in your story, article, or series of articles. No one knows query letters better than the master, Gordon Burgett, who's also my writing mentor. (Even experts need their own mentor.)

With special thanks to Gordon, here's his take on what makes a query letter work.

DOES YOUR QUERY PASS THESE FOUR TESTS?

1. Is it the kind of letter a professional would write?

The key word is *professional*. The letter must sound and look professional, with all the holes filled and all the information an editor will need to make a decision.

2. Is it brief, complete, clear, and positive?

BRIEF.　　　 Use no longer than a page to sell an article.

COMPLETE.　 A full page means a full page, not a sentence or graph.

CLEAR.　　　 It must be clear to the editor, not just to you.

POSITIVE.　　 You're trying to sell yourself and your consultancy.

3. Does it show attention to accuracy and detail?

Editors love both accuracy and detail, according to Gordon. I agree. As a colleague is fond of saying, "More specifics, please."

4. Is it convincing enough as to why the article should be written?

This is a sales (perish the thought) letter, not prose. While it's soft sell, if it's too soft, they won't know what you want. Remember the A-I-D-A sales formula: A for Attention; I for Interest; D for Desire; and A for Action step.

A SAMPLE LETTER

Here's a sample query letter. Though never actually sent, it includes all the elements of a good one.

Mr. Toby Smith

Editor

The Marketer Magazine

149 E. 33rd St.

New York City, NY 10000

Dear Mr. Smith:

Thomas Edison, Benjamin Franklin, Eli Whitney, Dr. Paul Winchell. Toshiro Nakamats?

No, that's not a typo. In fact, Dr. Toshiro Nakamats is more famous than all of these well-known inventors put together. In Japan, he's known as the "Edison of the far east."

Dr. Nakamats has over 4,000 patents, more than any other recorded by a human since patents began to be registered in 1788. Some of his more famous include a patent on the laser disk, the floppy disk drive, and the infamous porta-potty.

I've had the pleasure of meeting Dr. Nakamats, and I would like to share this experience—and some of Dr. Nakamats's vast knowledge—with your readers. Several months ago, he graciously agreed to sit for a three-hour interview.

Enclosed is an article based on that intensive session. We talked about many of his patents, from his very first at age 15 to his most recent one at age 71. Along the way, he discussed how the politics of Japanese management have both hindered and helped in the invention process. Unlike the United States, where inventors are on their own, in Japan inventors are free to create, knowing that their government is more than willing to subsidize their projects if they're good ones.

I'm offering you one-time North American serial rights to this fascinating man's thoughts, triumphs, and disappointments. All I ask in return is a byline and a resource box at the bottom of the article.

About me? I'm the author of four books, including *The Inventor's Marketing Handbook: A Complete Guide to Selling and Promoting Your Invention,* AAJA, 1989.

I've been in print over 100 times in various marketing and business journals, and I am currently editor of five medical marketing newsletters.

Don't worry about sending back the MS. Just your inventive response in the enclosed SASE will be enough.

Reece Franklin

APPENDIX 4

Working with the Media—from A to Z

Jan Norman and the *Orange County Register*

No method for getting your story published works all the time. The Associated Press says the average newsroom receives 122 press releases a day. More than 80 percent are tossed immediately because they are poorly written; are not presented in a suitable manner; lack information, content or interest; or are not news. But you can increase your chances for success. Here are some suggestions.

• **A**lways ask yourself how the reader will benefit from your information or story.

• **B**e mindful of deadlines. Some magazines must get information months in advance. Even daily newspapers need several days notice for everything but crisis news.

• **C**ontact names, phone numbers, fax numbers, and addresses should be put on every communication.

• **D**on't start your pitch by saying, "Write a story about my company." Tell the reporter what your story is.

- **E**liminate hype, self-praise, and unsupported claims from your releases.
- **F**ollow up releases with phone calls. Ask if you can provide anything else; how you can better meet the reporter's needs; if the release is not going to be used, why not?
- **G**etting into print is luck: that is, it's where preparation meets opportunity. So when the opportunity arises, be prepared.
- **H**aving the press keep track of your releases is futile; they're too busy. Don't ask them to keep you informed. It's up to you to keep track.
- **I**f you fax information, put the receiver's name on each page.
- **J**ust keep it short, please. Only stress what is newsworthy.
- **K**eep it simple, stupid. Write simple sentences. Follow the format used in any regular feature you target.
- *Largest, biggest, first, only,* etc.—claims you can't prove should never be made.
- **M**ake yourself an expert. Be available when reporters call for your expertise.
- **Never, ever lie to the press**
- **O**ne side of the page; one page per release, please.
- **P**roximity matters. Many pubs print only news from their circulation area.
- *Quiet* is the name of the game if you don't want people to know. There's no such thing as off-the-record.
- **R**ead target publications to learn where your info fits: new products, calendar, people briefs.
- **S**uggest art and chart opportunities for your story suggestion.
- **T**arget your efforts on pubs that reach your market.
- **U**pdate your list often; find out which editor or reporter to contact.
- **V**ery bad to try to bribe reporters or editors. Don't.
- **W**hen calling news people, ask first, "Are you on deadline? Is this a good time to talk?" Then keep it brief.
- **X**-rated: Telling a reporter "I want you to write an ad about my company."
- **Y**ou need to know what factors make a story newsworthy:

the unusual; proximity; prominence; people; crises; timeliness; impact.

• **Z**is is not news, mein friend: You've started a business (ho hum); your company is woman-owned (so are thousands of others); you've stayed in biz one year (call me when you hit 25); your business is profitable (isn't that the reason you went in business, anyway?).

Note: List by Jan Norman of the *Orange County Register.* Adaptation by the author.

APPENDIX 5

Case Histories

CASE HISTORY 1:1 FREEDOM TO FLY

SITUATION

This client came from a student who took a marketing class of mine back in 1990. She was the bookkeeper for a psychologist who had just teamed up with a pilot friend to produce an audio-tape, "Overcoming Your Fear of Flying." After she introduced me to her boss, he hired us to do a campaign to generate word of mouth and publicity for the audiotape. My suggestion of putting a book out was not heeded; instead, the client spent thousands on a videotape (it was the pilot's money). An audiotape based on the video sold much better (lower price). This client did get coverage through two major newspaper syndicates; eventually, the tape was picked up by a major catalog, Sybervision.

WHO	Psychologist specializing in phobias
	Senior pilot for major airline
WHAT	Consultants to individuals and companies on overcoming your fear of flying
WHEN	Late 1991 to mid 1992
WHERE	National campaign
WHY	Over 45 million American travelers are afraid to fly. FREEDOM TO FLY was established to help these people overcome their fears.
METHODS	Press kit, including releases, backgrounder, fact sheet, author bio, photos
	Giant PR Postcard for Radio Campaign
	Audiotapes/Videotapes—samples and products
	College workshops
	Speeches
RESULTS	Major release picked up verbatim by Scripps–Howard syndicate; several Gannett papers.
	Radio "hot card" blitz generated several dozen radio interviews.
	Audiotape series picked up by Sybervision for catalog.
	Review in *Library Journal* and *Publishers Weekly*

CASE HISTORY 2:1 SURVIVE ALIVE INDUSTRIES

WHO	Land Surveyor, owner of two-man company
WHAT	Reposition as earthquake consultant;
	Sell earthquake kit products
WHEN	1992
WHERE	Local campaign
WHY	Dozens of earthquakes hit Southern California every year. Client wanted to sell earthquake kits, jump on bandwagon.

METHODS	Complete repositioning of client into earthquake "expert."
	Booklet written by client showing easy step method for surviving an earthquake.
	Company named.
	Products researched, packaging designed.
	Campaign included: Press kit, including releases, backgrounder, fact sheet, photos.
	Giant PR postcard for radio campaign (local)
RESULTS	Interviews on local ABC, NBC, CBS affiliates in hometown
	Major papers in hometown ran story on the local expert.
	Los Angeles radio and TV media did quick interviews after another aftershock hit.
	Largest school association in state used as vendor for products.

SITUATION

This was a client who, in hindsight, I really shouldn't have taken on. He wanted to jump on the bandwagon and sell earthquake kits and supplies in South California. With over 155 earthquake-kit vendors in the Los Angeles basin and with his company located 200 miles north of L.A., the positioning angle was wrong. Added to that, he worked full time running his other company, so he couldn't devote the effort that the campaign or sales needed. It wasn't the most promising of situations. Still, we did manage to get him coverage on a major Los Angeles TV station as an "out-of-town expert." He also got radio coverage in L.A. In his hometown, however, he's considered something of an earthquake guru. This goes to show you, always start local—and sometimes stay there.

CASE HISTORY 3:1 ABP PUBLISHERS

WHO   Human resources manager/consultant
             Former aerospace employee
WHAT   Book entitled *Yes, There Is Life after Aerospace*
WHEN   Late 1994
WHERE   National campaign
WHY   Over 3 million American aerospace workers have been laid off in the last several years. The author is a consultant who gives seminars on career adjustment for these individuals. The book was written to increase (1) back-of-the-room (BOR) sales and (2) the author's market and visibility to the industry.
METHODS   Press kit, including releases, backgrounder, fact sheet, author bio, photos
             Giant PR postcard for radio campaign
             Actual $8\frac{1}{2} \times 11\frac{1}{2}$ book—160-page paperback
             College workshops
             Speeches
RESULTS   Major release picked up by local regional newspapers—three columns wide by length of paper (approx. $2,000 worth of space); Radio "hot card" blitz generated several dozen radio interviews.

CASE HISTORY 4:1 NATIONAL INVENTORS' DAY

WHO   Reece Franklin, author of *Inventor's Marketing Handbook*
WHAT   Campaign to help launch my first book and position me as an expert in invention marketing.
WHEN   1989–92
WHERE   Local, regional, national campaign

WHY	Inventors are frustrated by lack of understanding how marketing process works. Too many books on general marketing; nothing niched for them. Campaign must position me as the expert against five other inventors' books coming out simultaneously.
METHODS	He with the most publicity wins. Used: Author's press kit, incl. bio, backgrounder, reviewer's fact sheet, release, photo, book cover as jacket, Q-and-A. Standard release; radio "hot card" blitz; follow-up phone calls.
RESULTS	Radio "hot card" generated 28 radio talk shows within three weeks. Release and follow-up calls using local angle generated 27 stories for 1.2 million circulation within three weeks.

SCENARIOS

In 1989 I wrote the *Inventor's Marketing Handbook*. That year five other books also on invention marketing came out. I positioned myself using the colonial costume of Ben Franklin, as described earlier in this book.

In 1990, while in New York at the American Booksellers' Convention, I met the then associate book editor for the *Los Angeles Times Book Review* section. At home, I sent her a copy with a note saying this would be a great story to tie in with the 1990 Invention Convention. She liked my idea and ran the story two days before the show.

Also in 1990, I got the idea to do a quick "blitz" campaign around the angle of Thomas Edison's birthday. Three years earlier it had been designated National Inventors' Day by a local Washington, D.C. club—and then forgotten.

I recoined the phrase and sent a PR hot card to Joe Sabah's list of radio stations, talking about February 11 being National Inventors' Day that *should be.*

My releases and pitches were all "semicustomized" for each area. The concept was the same for each—I wanted President Bush to declare February 11 National Inventors' Day. (I'm still working on it, five years later. Washington moves slowly, I'm afraid.)

If the publication stated they needed a local angle, I tried to come up with one. Barring that, I tried to find local inventors in their areas who agreed with me. In total, I got 27 stories and 28 radio interviews in a little under three weeks. (In hindsight, I should definitely have given myself more time: I created the angle February 1. Not bad results for ten days' work—with very little sleep!)

I tried to customize the releases, as I suggest in this book. In this case, I really didn't have time. I did, however, take one paragraph per release and change it.

Since I knew that 50 percent of the U.S. population are wanna-be inventors (my source: U.S. Patent and Trademark Office), I took the population of each newspaper's area of influence and divided the population in half. Then I started each release with the numbers. For example: "30,000 Chinoites are wanna-be inventors," according to Reece Franklin, local author who is lobbying to have Congress declare February 11 National Inventors' Day.

For your further education, here are some of the angles I pitched, along with the headline change in the release.

NEWSPAPER	PITCH ANGLE
La Habra Star Progress	"Former La Habran Lobbies for National Inventors' Day" (I lived there when I wrote the book)
Chino Hills Champion	"Local Author Lobbies for Inventors' Day" (I live there now)
Pomona Progress Bulletin	We consider ourselves part of the Pomona Valley—local again

CASE HISTORIES

NEWSPAPER	PITCH ANGLE
San Bernardino Sun	I live in S.B. County (local)
Northern Ill. Univ. Star	"Alumnus Lobbies for National Day"
Bakersfield Californian	I teach an inventor's class there, and pitched story prior to my arrival (regional)
Orange Coast Daily Pilot	"OCC Teacher to Honor Inventors" (see explanation below)

While I don't have time to discuss all 27 hits, suffice it to say the blitz idea works. (My thanks to my friend Dr. Jeffrey Lant for inventing this idea, known as the *media wave*. Now when someone says "make waves," you know what they mean.)

A final, parting note on this campaign. While it generated several dozen book orders, it also positioned me as the expert. I've used it to sell the book rights for the third printing to a major California publishing house and to show credibility to many new clients and friends.

But the funniest thing was it actually taught me something—how to "localize" a story when there isn't a local angle. You see, every editor and reporter wants that "scoop," that exclusive. That's why they're always looking for the local angle.

I'd done most of the pitching, and I decided to try south Orange County, home of the *Register* and the *Daily Pilot*. The *Pilot* editor kept saying, "It's a great story, Reece, but it's not local enough." Even when I mentioned local inventors he could talk to, he kept turning me down. Finally, in desperation I remarked "Well, I teach at Orange Coast College. Is that local enough?" Bingo!! He bit. He mentioned that each Monday the paper featured a story on a local educator. Did I want next Monday's half-page spread? Did I want it? You bet!

APPENDIX 6

Media Contact List

NATIONAL NEWSPAPERS OF INTEREST TO CONSULTANTS

Arizona Republic
120 East Van Buren
Phoenix, AZ 85004
(602) 271-8000

Asbury Park Press
3601 Highway 66
Neptune, NJ 07754
(908) 922-6000

Atlanta Constitution
Atlanta Journal
72 Marietta St. NW
Atlanta, GA 30303
(404) 526-5151

Baltimore Sun
501 North Calvert St.
P.O. Box 1377
Baltimore, MD 21278
(410) 332-6000

Boston Globe
135 Morrison Blvd.
Boston, MA 02107
(617) 929-2000

Boston Herald
P.O. Box 2096
Boston, MA 02106
(617) 426-3000

Chicago Sun Times
401 North Wabash
Chicago, IL 60611
(312) 321-3000

Chicago Tribune
435 North Michigan Ave.
Chicago, IL 60611
(312) 222-3232

Cincinnati Enquirer
312 Elm St.
Cincinnati, OH 45202
(513) 721-2700

Deborah
Jordan —

523 - 3037

MEDIA CONTACT LIST

Cincinnati Post
125 East Court St.
Cincinnati, OH 45202
(513) 352-2000

Cleveland
Plain Dealer
1801 Superior Ave. NE
Cleveland, OH 44114
(216) 999-4800

Dallas Morning News
P.O. Box 655237
Dallas, TX 75265
(214) 977-8222

Daytona Beach News-
Journal
901 Sixth St.
Daytona Beach, FL 32117
(904) 252-1511

Denver Post
1560 Broadway
Denver, CO 80202
(303) 820-1010

Detroit Free Press
326 West Lafayette
Detroit, MI 48231
(313) 222-6400

Detroit News
615 West Lafayette
Detroit, MI 48231
(313) 222-2300

Fort Worth
Star-Telegram
400 West Seventh St.
Fort Worth, TX 76101
(817) 390-7400

Hartford Courant
285 Broad St.
Hartford, CT 06115
(203) 241-6200

Honolulu
Star-Bulletin
605 Kapiolani Blvd.
Honolulu, HI 96802
(808) 525-8000

Houston Chronicle
801 Texas Ave.
Houston, TX 77002
(713) 220-7171

Indianapolis Star-News
307 North Pennsylvania St.
Indianapolis, IN 46204
(317) 633-1240

Kansas City Star
1729 Grand Blvd.
Kansas City, MO 64108
(816) 234-4141

Los Angeles Times
Times Mirror Square
Los Angeles, CA 90053
(213) 237-5000

Memphis Commercial
Appeal
495 Union Ave.
Memphis, TN 38103
(901) 529-2211

Miami Herald
One Herald Plaza
Miami, FL 33132
(305) 350-2111

Milwaukee
Journal-Sentinel
333 West State St.
Milwaukee, WI 53201
(414) 224-2000

Minneapolis
Star-Tribune
425 Portland Ave.
Minneapolis, MN 55488
(612) 673-4000

New Haven Register
40 Sargent Dr.
New Haven, CT 06511
(203) 789-5200

New Orleans Times
Picayune-States Item
3800 Howard Ave.
New Orleans, LA 70125
(504) 826-3279

Newsday
235 Pinelawn Rd.
Melville, NY 11747
(516) 454-2020

New York Daily News
220 East 42d St.
New York, NY 10017
(212) 210-2100

New York Post
210 South St.
New York, NY 10002
(212) 815-8000

New York Times
229 West 43d St.
New York, NY 10036
(212) 556-1234

MEDIA CONTACT LIST

Orange County
Register
625 North Grand Ave.
Santa Ana, CA 92701
(714) 835-1234

Orlando Sentinel
633 North Orange Ave.
P.O. Box 2833
Orlando, FL 32802
(407) 420-5000

Philadelphia Inquirer
Philadelphia Daily News
400 Broad St.
Philadelphia, PA 19130
(215) 854-2000
(215) 854-5900

Pittsburgh
Post-Gazette
34 Boulevard of Allies
Pittsburgh, PA 15222
(412) 263-1100

Portand Oregonian
1320 Southwest Broadway
Portland, OR 97201
(503) 221-8327

Rocky Mountain News
400 West Colfax
Denver, CO 80204
(303) 892-5000

Sacramento Bee
2100 Q Street
Sacramento, CA 95816
(916) 321-1000

Salt Lake City Tribune
P.O. Box 867
Salt Lake City, UT 84110
(801) 237-2011

San Diego
Union-Tribune
350 Camino de la Reina
San Diego, CA 92108
(619) 299-3131

San Francisco
Chronicle
901 Mission
San Francisco, CA 94103
(415) 777-1111

San Francisco
Examiner
110 Fifth St.
San Francisco, CA 94103
(415) 777-2424

Seattle
Post-Intelligencer
101 Elliott Ave. W
Seattle, WA 98111
(206) 448-8000

Seattle Times
1120 John St.
Seattle, WA 98111
(206) 464-2111

St. Louis Post-Dispatch
900 North Tucker Blvd.
St. Louis, MO 63101
(314) 340-8000

St. Paul Pioneer Press
345 Cedar St.
St. Paul, MN 55101
(612) 222-5011

St. Petersburg Times
490 First Ave. S
St. Petersburg, FL 33731
(813) 893-8111

Tacoma News-Tribune
1950 South State
P.O. Box 1100
Tacoma, WA 98405
(206) 597-8742

Tampa Tribune
202 South Parker St.
Tampa, FL 33606
(813) 272-7600

USA Today
1000 Wilson Blvd.
Arlington, VA 22229
(703) 276-3400

*The Wall Street
Journal*
200 Liberty St.
New York, NY 10281
(212) 416-2000

Washington Post
1150 15th St. NW
Washington, DC 20071
(202) 334-6000

Washington Times
3600 New York Ave. NE
Washington, DC 20002
(202) 636-3000

MAGAZINES OF INTEREST TO CONSULTANTS

American Legion
P.O. Box 1055
Indianapolis, IN 46206
(317) 630-1200

Barron's
420 Lexington Ave.
New York, NY 10170
(212) 808-7200

*Broadcasting
and Cable*
1705 DeSales St. NW
Washington, DC 20036
(202) 659-2340

Business Marketing
740 Rush St.
Chicago, IL 60611
(312) 649-5260

Business Week
1221 Avenue of the Americas
New York, NY 10020
(212) 512-2511

Direct Marketing
224 Seventh St.
Garden City, NY 11530
(516) 746-6700

Entrepreneur
2392 Morse Ave.
Irvine, CA 92714
(714) 261-2325

Forbes
60 Fifth Ave.
New York, NY 10011
(212) 620-2200

Fortune
Time-Life Bldg.
New York, NY 10020
(212) 586-1212

Inc.
38 Commercial Wharf
Boston, MA 02110
(617) 248-8000

Life
Time-Life Bldg.
New York, NY 10020
(212) 586-1212

Modern Maturity
3200 East Carson St.
Lakewood, CA 90712
(310) 496-2277

Money
Time-Life Bldg.
New York, NY 10020
(212) 586-1212

Ms.
230 Park Ave.
New York, NY 10169
(212) 551-9595

Newsweek
251 West 57th St.
New York, NY 10019
(212) 445-4000

New Yorker
25 West 43d St.
New York, NY 10036
(212) 840-3800

People
Time-Life Bldg.
New York, NY 10020
(212) 586-1212

Playboy
680 N. Lake Shore Dr.
Chicago, IL 60611
(312) 751-8000

Reader's Digest
Reader's Digest Rd.
Pleasantville, NY 10570
(914) 238-1000

Sales and Marketing Management
870 Belleville Dr.
Valley Cottage, NY 10989
(914) 268-5120

Time
Time-Life Bldg.
New York, NY 10020
(212) 586-1212

U.S. News and World Report
2400 N St. NW
Washington, DC 20037
(202) 955-2000

WIRE SERVICES

Associated Press
50 Rockefeller Plaza
New York, NY 10020
(212) 621-1500

College Press Service
64 East Concord St.
Orlando, FL 32801
(407) 839-5754

Copley News Service
123 Camino de la Reina
San Diego, CA 92112
(619) 293-1818

Gannett News Service
1000 Wilson Blvd.
Arlington, VA 22209
(703) 276-5800

King Features
Syndicate
235 East 45th St.
New York, NY 10017
(212) 455-4000

Knight-Ridder
75 Wall St.
New York, NY 10005
(212) 269-1110

New York Times News
Service
229 West 43d St.
New York, NY 10036
(212) 556-1927

Reuters
1700 Broadway
New York, NY 10019
(212) 603-3300

Scripps-Howard
News Service
1090 Vermont Ave. NW
Washington, DC 20036
(202) 408-1484

United Press
International
2 Penn Plaza
New York, NY 10121
(212) 560-1100

NATIONAL TELEVISION NEWS AND TALK SHOWS

CBS This Morning
51 West 52d St.
New York, NY 10019
(212) 975-4321

CNN
One CNN Center
Atlanta, GA 30348
(404) 827-1500

Fox Broadcasting
10201 West Pico Blvd.
Los Angeles, CA 90035
(213) 462-7111

Good Morning
America
77 West 66th St.
New York, NY 10023
(212) 456-7777

PBS
1320 Braddock Pl.
Alexandria, VA 22314
(703) 739-5000

Today
30 Rockefeller Plaza
New York, NY 10112
(212) 664-4444

USA Network
1230 Avenue of the Americas
New York, NY 10020
(212) 408-9100

RADIO NETWORKS

AP Radio
1825 K St. NW, Ste. 710
Washington, DC 20006
(202) 736-1100

National Public Radio (NPR)
635 Massachusetts Ave. NW
Washington, DC 20001
(202) 414-2000

UPI Radio Network
1400 I St. NW
Washington, DC 20005
(202) 898-8111

APPENDIX 7

Publicity Resource List

BOOK REVIEWERS

Bloomsbury Review
1028 Bannock St.
Denver, CO 80204

Book List
American Library Association
50 East Huron St.
Chicago, IL 60611
(312) 944-6780

Bookwatch
166 Miramar Ave.
San Francisco, CA 94112

Chicago Tribune Books
435 N. Michigan Ave.
Chicago, IL 60611-4022

Choice
100 Riverview Center
Middletown, CT 06457
(203) 347-6933

Kirkus Reviews
200 Park Ave. South
New York, NY 10003-1543

Library Journal
249 West 17th St.
New York, NY 10011
(212) 463-6822

New York Review of Books
250 West 57th St.
New York, NY 10107-0001
(212) 757-8070

New York Times Book Review
229 West 57th St.
New York, NY 10036

Publishers Weekly
249 W. 17th St.
New York, NY 10011
(212) 645-0067

San Francisco Review of Books
Box 33-0090
San Francisco, CA 94133

DIRECTORIES IMPORTANT TO CONSULTANTS

Gale Research Company
835 Penobscot Bldg.
Detroit, MI 48226
(800) 877-4253

- Association Periodicals Directory

- Business, Organizations, Agencies, and Publications
- City and State Directories In Print

- Consultants Directory

- Contemporary Authors

- Directories In Print

- Directory of Publications and Broadcast Media

- Encyclopedia of Associations

- Encyclopedia of Business Information Sources

- Newsletters in Print

Yearbook of Experts, Authorities, and Spokespersons
Mitchell P. Davis, Editor
Broadcast Interview Source
2233 Wisconsin Ave. NW
Washington, DC 20007
(800) 955-0311

MEDIA DIRECTORIES

Bacon's Publicity Checker
332 S. Michigan Ave.
Chicago, IL 60604
(800) 621-0561

BPI: BPI Media Services
1515 Broadway
New York, NY 10036
(800) 284-4915

Broadcasting/Cablecasting
Yearbook
1705 DeSales St. NW
Washington, DC 20036

Burelle's Media Info
75 E. Northfield Rd.
Livingston, NJ 07039
(800) 631-1160

California Publishing
Marketplace
Writer's Connection
275 Saratoga Ave.
Santa Clara, CA 95050
(408) 554-2090

Directory of Texas Markets
c/o Dana Cassell
Maple Ridge Rd.
North Sandwich, NH 03259
(603) 284-6367

Directory of Women's Media
530 Broadway, 10th Fl.
New York, NY 10021
(212) 570-5001

Larami Media Guides
5 W. 37th St.
New York, NY 10018

Literary Market Place
Reed Reference Publications
121 Chanlon Rd.
New Providence, NJ 07974

Power Media Selects
Broadcast Interview Source
2233 Wisconsin Ave. NW
Washington DC 20007
(202) 333-4904

Standard Periodical Directory
Oxbridge Directory of
Newsletters
Oxbridge Communications
150 Fifth Ave.
New York, NY 10011
(212) 741-0231

Ulrich's Int'l. Periodicals
Directory and
Working Press of the Nation
R.R. Bowker Company
121 Chanlon Rd.
New Providence, NJ 07974
(800) 521-8110

Writer's Market
Writer's Digest Books
1507 Dana Ave.
Cincinnati, OH 45207
(800) 543-4644

Writer's Northwest Handbook
Media Weavers
24450 N.W. Hansen Rd.
Hillsboro, OR 97124
(503) 621-3911

Writers Resource
Guide/Seattle
Writers Publishing Service
1512 Western Ave.
Seattle, WA 98101
(206) 467-6735

NEWSLETTERS

These subscription newsletters
list the new columns, shows,
magazines, and what they're
looking for:

Bulldog Reporter
1250 45th St., Ste.200
Emeryville, CA 94608
(510) 596-9300

Contacts
3520 Broadway
Astoria, NY 11106-1114
(718) 721-0508

Partyline
35 Sutton Pl.
New York, NY 10022
(212) 755-3487

ORGANIZATIONS

Book Publicists of Southern
California
6464 Sunset Blvd.
Hollywood, CA 90028
(213) 461-3921

COSMEP
International Association of
Independent
Publishers
Box 420703
San Francisco, CA 94142
(415) 922-9490

Publishers Marketing
Association
2401 P.C.H. #102
Hermosa Beach, CA 90254
(310) 372-2732

American Booksellers
Association
560 White Plains Rd.
Tarrytown, NY 10591
(800) 637-0037

PLACES TO PITCH DIRECTORIES

Radio-TV Interview Report
135 E. Plumstead Ave.
Landsdowne, PA 19050
(215) 259-1070

Bimonthly magazine sent to over 5,000 talk-show and TV news programming executives in the U.S.

Publicity Express
1563 Solano Ave., No. 223
Berkeley, CA 94707
(800) 541-2897

Monthly magazine mailed to over 5,000 electronic media.

PR Newswire (PRN)
150 E. 38th St.
New York, NY 10155
(800) 832-5522

Daily service providing news releases and camera-ready photo transmissions to large media network via satellite, etc.

Audio TV Features
149 Madison Ave.
New York, NY 10016
(212) 889-1342

Daily radio service feeds 2,000 news and talk radio stations and all AP and UPI wire service subscribers

North American Precis
Syndicate
4209 Vantage Ave.
Studio City, CA 91604
(818) 761-8400

Monthly distributor of multimedia script and slide packages to 3,000+ radio and TV news and talk shows.

Derus Media
500 N. Dearborn, No. 516
Chicago, IL 60601
(312) 644-4360

Monthly distribution of script and slide packages to radio

and TV outlets. Also in the Hispanic market.

News USA
2300 Claredon Blvd.
Arlington, VA 22201
(800) 868-6872

Distributes releases editorial features, and camera-ready art to 10,000+ newspapers.

Metro Publicity Services
33 W. 34th St.
New York, NY 10001
(212) 947-5100

Mails monthly to 7,000 newspapers. Theme sections for targeted audiences 22 times per year.

PUBLIC RELATIONS COMPANIES

O'Dwyer's Directory of Public Relations
J. R. O'Dwyer Co.
271 Madison Ave.
New York, NY 10016
(212) 679-2471

VIDEO NEWS RELEASES

A video news release (VNR) is basically a press release in video form, typically a 90-second piece that is paid for by a sponsor and distributed via satellite around the country to TV stations to be included in local newscasts.

Medialink
708 Third Ave.
New York, NY 10017
(212) 682-8300

1401 New York Ave. NW, Ste. 520
Washington, DC 20005
(202) 628-3800

6430 Sunset Blvd.
Los Angeles, CA 90028
(213) 465-0111

541 N. Fairbanks Ct.
Chicago, IL 60611
(312) 222-9850

APPENDIX 8

Interview with Jan Norman

No one I know in the media deals more with consultants on a daily basis than my friend Jan Norman, small-business reporter for the *Orange County Register.* To gain insight into what editors and reporters think about us, I interviewed her at her office in early 1995.

REECE FRANKLIN: How do you define the difference between publicity and public relations?

JAN NORMAN: I don't think reporters make that kind of distinction. And I think consultants and business owners need to appreciate that. We may not be able to speak the jargon that they learn in a class or that they might learn on their own. They see this distinction.

What we're looking for would tend to be audience. If something is too much like "I am a swell business" or "I am a swell person," we would see that as being more of a free ad, and reporters get real tense out of doing that type of thing for businesses.

On the other hand, we see as absolutely vital people who can be resources on subjects that are of interest to our readers. Or if you're in television, the same would be true of our viewers, because we also do features for our Orange County News Channel.

So what *we're* looking for is the audience point of view, whereas the consultant is going to be looking to "get my name out in front of the public." Now, all the consultant needs to do is turn that around, so that the way he or she is saying it tends to be "Gee, this is what's in it for the audience"—when actually the secret thing going on is the give-back to him or her, the "My name gets out in front of the public."

REECE: But aren't there two audiences? There's the editor/reporter, then there's the ultimate audience, which is the reader. So doesn't the consultant need to know both audiences?

JAN: But how different is the editor or reporter? Sure, we all carry our own baggage of personal likes and dislikes and prejudices, but we are kind of a filter because we can't put absolutely everything of interest out there. If I've got ten interesting things, which is going to be of most significance? What most reporters are doing is putting themselves in the reader's shoes. "Gee, I'm interested in this; gee, I need to know this." And so we aren't that different in what we're looking for; we're just being the buyer of information for our readers.

REECE: So if the consultant understands the reporter or electronic media's readers, listeners, or viewers—and can write so it's of interest to them—then it makes sense for you to pick it up.

JAN: Right, and that's where it gets real tricky with audiences—for example, the audience for a very technical journal. Let's say you're a computer consultant and you're targeting a magazine whose audience with their average years in computer experience would be ten years—your level of sophistication is going to be very different than if the target audience is a general publication newspaper, where the average reader may be lucky to own a computer. So then, **the consultant needs to think in terms of what the**

audience needs to know, how much do they already know? [Emphasis mine—Reece.]

Tailor their writing to the particular audience. The consultant can target both audiences; he just needs to be sure he doesn't confuse them. You don't want the editor to say, "Our readers already know that" in the case of the technical journal. Or in the case of the general newspaper, the editor saying, "That's too technical for *our* readers." Then start looking where to place that within a publication.

REECE: Is there a real thin line between what reporters like yourself consider advertising vs. a story, or is it a little broader?

JAN: I think there are real black-and-white cases, and then there are cases of gray. I'm a business reporter, so I'm not as adverse to someone saying, "My business is as a consultant." But where I'd be willing to put that in the newspaper, there might be other reporters who don't write about business, who just think that's the worst thing they could possibly do. They love to quote government bureaucrats and academics but don't realize the value of people who're out there in business. And consultants need to appreciate those kinds of biases in the editors and reporters they're pitching.

REECE: How do they know about the biases? How can they tell?

JAN: Well, you don't. You pay attention to what they put in the paper. If you notice that a particular publication never quotes anyone in private business, there probably is a bias. Another point being: You should study a publication before you pitch them. I'm always amazed at people who will call me up and pitch me on ideas or a column I've done just two weeks prior or on the type of thing I'd never write about. For example, if you have a new product, you have to find out who writes about new products. Because even if you've got the right publication, you've got to target the right person.

Let's get back to this bias people might have about saying "I'll never quote a person in business." I think we're overcoming that to some extent. I find more and more reporters coming to me and asking, "Do you have an expert on xyz?" And I will have within my database ten people knowledgeable on that subject. But what happens on most papers is that you get a big staff turnover. So you may have cultivated a reporter who knows your expertise, and that person leaves the publication; then you may no longer have any contact inside that paper. It's a continuing process. And the next person in may have a different set of biases. So it's a continuing process, finding out what each person prefers.

One thing that I find so very interesting is that I'll tell a reporter about a story that I find fascinating, and they'll cover that particular beat and think it's just awful. Some of it has to do with what we find interesting.

REECE: That, I think, is one of the biggest problems for anyone. How do you know what will interest a reporter and an editor? You really don't, do you?

JAN: Sometimes it depends on how it's pitched. I was thinking about this the other day, because there's a product on the market—it's a kids product. When I was pitched for that, I didn't have a lot of interest. It had to do with the fact that my kid is grown. But at the time that Playmate Toys came out with Teenage Mutant Ninja Turtles, my son was younger so I had an appreciation for how big that whole thing was.

You don't know the reporter; all you can do is be honest with the story that you have and always keep in mind the reader. Say "Here's what's in it for the reader," so even if the reporter is biased, if you can show popularity, then you can show a potential audience for the story.

REECE: Let's talk about pitching a reporter. In my classes I teach students to pitch on the phone first to see if there's an interest before sending the release. And then follow up with the phone call. Should it be done that way, or is it better to send out many releases, followed up with a round of calls?

JAN: People do it both ways with me, and because of that, I have to give some attention to how I personally react. And I know different reporters want it different ways. I have found that what works best with me is getting that initial phone call saying it's coming. I get so much mail that if I don't get that call, I might miss it. If I know something's coming, I'll at least take the additional time to look at it. And then the person can follow it up again.

It can't hurt to make the call. If you call a person and they say, "Don't call me again, just send it," you've at least alerted them it's coming. I tend to think it's better to call first and say, "Is this suitable for you?" Then if it's not, they can at least send you to another reporter.

Also, if it's someone you're going to pitch on a continuing basis, and they don't want a phone call first but want it in the mail, just make that note on your card file.

But I'm just telling you what works for me. And anyone who gets a huge volume of mail will probably work the same way.

REECE: Now, does the word *consultant* turn reporters off?

JAN: Because of the work I do with small business, I've come to appreciate what consultants do. I really can't speak for all reporters. I know that it helps me to know what you're a consultant in. If you can be more specific about what you're a consultant in— not just "a computer consultant" but "high technology about xyz"—that helps.

Consultants tend to know quite a bit about their industry. They can give me background about their whole industry because they tend to study their own industries and have a sense of their size. For most business reporters, it's not a back-off, vampire case. For nonbusiness reporters, there might be that stigma.

REECE: So, should consultants be targeting business reporters only?

JAN: It depends on your story. Let's say your story has to do with naming products or new product research. That type of thing might be pitched very effectively to someone in the feature section. Human-behavior types of stories. A lot of consultants will pitch the business sections, and a lot of business sections in newspapers are different than they were even ten years ago. They're evolving more quickly, trying to be more consumer oriented. So that's not something where you would say, "Oh, I don't want to be there anymore." If, for example, you're a consultant—say earthquake preparedness—you need to be working with the reporter who probably covers science or earthquakes. You need to be mindful that the person isn't a business reporter and try to approach them with "here's what's in it for the reader." Bearing in mind that this person is a techie or science kind of person rather than a dollars-and-cents business kind of reporter. If you're doing health care— the *Register*'s structured very much this way—the health care reporters are supposed to be able to do the business side of health care as much as the human-caring kinds, but that isn't always the case. So you need to play to that reporter's strength. If you notice that the health care reporter is always doing stories about scientific breakthroughs, you have a hint that he is more of a science kind of person and needs to be approached as a science kind of person. If the stories tend to be more about the business of science, you need to approach him that way.

REECE: And that's finding out by doing that homework and reading . . .

JAN: Right, reading that publication first.

REECE: So would you suggest a month, two months, six months back?

JAN: Yeah. At least two or three months. And for some re-porters, because they print just one or two stories every couple of weeks, you might need to go back even further.

REECE: You're one of the most open and accessible reporters I've met. Yet reporters in various regions of the country, like the south United States, seem not to be as open as in other areas to new ideas and consultants. Your fellow colleagues that you've talked to over the years, are they as open as you are?

JAN: Maybe it's because of my personality, maybe it's because of what I cover—I probably am more accessible. I don't know how you overcome that. Some reporters, I don't see how they can be reporters, they're so closed to new ideas. The reason I'm accessible is that it opens my eyes to things that I wouldn't know if I didn't have sources.

REECE: How should a consultant approach a business reporter?

JAN: There's a whole thing in marketing about "sell the benefits, not the features." Lead with what the story is—cut to the chase. If your pitch letter is more than a page long, you're really pushing it. You've got to hone that sentence saying, "If you don't have this story, your readers will suffer." But it's got to be all to the benefit of what you have to offer. Who you are—and your credentials to be a source for that particular story—is secondary. You've got to convince them that you've got a story. A must-write-about trend. Go with what the story is. It doesn't matter as much who you are as what you can deliver.

REECE: You mention the pitch letter. Should one go with just a release, a pitch letter prior to the release, or both?

JAN: That's interesting. I get them both ways. It's a mixed bag. The criticism I have with releases is that the first sentence doesn't tell me a benefit. Too often they start off with the feature leads, and the whole point is buried someplace. Your release should have in that first sentence what it is my readers are going to find most interesting—same thing would be true of a pitch letter—start off with why I should care. Because if the only thing I read is that first sentence, if it's fluff I won't read any further.

REECE: What if a consultant really doesn't have an exciting story to talk about? All they have is opening an office and so on. Most reporters don't want that stuff, do they?

JAN: Well, there are places where that fits. The *Register* has a People on the Move section. That will get them about one sentence. People who think they'll get a twelve-inch feature because they moved into a new office—I mean, those days are gone! A one-sentence "XYZ moved to new offices" is all it requires.

But if you don't have a story idea, you're not thinking hard enough. Or maybe try another line of work.

REECE: What if a consultant is not in a high-tech line of work, does that make a difference?

JAN: No. But that's where a lot of them are.

Let me think of some unusual consultants. I've met with consultants who work with companies when they're changing their names. Real fertile field for interesting stuff for daily newspapers, let alone technical journals. Things like brand-name identification and the psychology of naming a product. That consumers find interesting.

So often when you're a high-tech consultant, it's the human element that really draws people in. The drama—the crashing into defeat and rising from the ashes—makes a wonderful story. And lots of times the most successful consultants who pitch me are really telling me success stories of their clients.

The consultant has to realize that his job is to be a conduit for these clients. Sometimes they themselves might just be a secondary source in a story that winds up being a lot about their client. And that's where consultants can really shine, because they've become the expert on the client's product. They then become that unbiased source of expertise, that voice of authority, even though the story's not about them. You'd be surprised how many people will call that consultant from a story like that, based on "Oh, gee, he must be an expert, he must know what he's talking about because he helped that company survive."

Always be looking, if you don't have a story to tell, at what your clients have done. That may be the human-interest angle I'm looking for.

REECE: How much do reporters trust the accuracy of the statistics quoted? You don't do your own checking, do you?

JAN: Sometimes. Or if some people tell me the source. And more and more there are ways of doing that checking, through your local reference librarian or on the Internet. All kinds of ways of getting useful statistics—trade shows, for example. If you're throwing out a statistic and you think I'm not going to trust it, tell me where you got it.

REECE: OK, how often do you yourself check these statistics, irregularly or regularly?

JAN: Pretty regularly. Or at least I'll ask the source where they got it.

REECE: How would you suggest consultants stretch their mind to get story ideas?

JAN: Well, one thing—you've got to be realistic—is that not every story is going to fly. Another possibility is to look at other publications from other locations that maybe have done a similar kind of story that can be adapted to your own situation.

Don't insist on the story being on just your client. For example, if your client is in a particular industry, is there some industry-wide trend that you can make reference to. Or your own industry.

REECE: Does it help if consultants attach a clip sheet?

JAN: It's risky, based on the geographic area of the publications. For example, anytime someone sends me a copy of a story that ran in the *L.A. Times,* I toss it out. Because the *L.A. Times* and the *Register* are so competitive that there's no way one of them will be interested in following up on a story that was in a competitor. The way it might help: If I'm doing a story on toy trends and your company has been featured in another publication, that may be OK if it's a different tack than I'm taking. But if it's the same story, I don't want to know that I've been beaten on the story. [Note to readers: Customize those releases—Reece.] Using a clip sheet to establish your credibility and longevity is one thing; using it as a do-me-too is pretty risky.

REECE: What type of stories turns your fire on?

JAN: People stories. Overcoming adversity. Where people can relate to the problems. It's more of a triumph—someone who went through the fire and came through.

REECE: When do you recommend people send you press kits? I tell my students, "When they ask you for them, send them. If they don't, don't."

JAN: That's right. And one of the best things would be a Rolodex card or a way to show your expertise on the business cards. I put my sources on computer database. So list your areas of expertise. When I need that expertise, I will do a search. So put it on your business cards. The more things you can do that don't hurt you, the better the chance that one of them may help. But it has to be done more quickly than a complete press kit can do it.

REECE: If you can sum this up, how do you best deal with a reporter?

JAN: Don't ever burn a reporter because if you do they will never use one of your stories again, and they will pass the word around. If you're double planting [pitching two reporters at the same publication], let them know. But if you tell me something that isn't true, if you promise a story that is less than what was claimed, you've undermined your credibility, and I'll never use you again. Or I'll be very cautious.

Another thing to do: Let them know you're accessible. You've done a lot of cultivation to let a reporter know you're an expert in a particular field. So one of the best things you can do in cultivating a long-term relationship once you've done all that hard work, is keep in touch. And know the deadlines so you get back immediately. So meet my deadlines, and call me back. Be sensitive to those kinds of things so you can make their job easier.

Another thing about consultants: Let people know where you are. Don't have a flat recording; let them know exactly where you're at.

REECE: How many sources are there on your database? And how does a consultant get to be the top one or two on the list?

JAN: I have over 2,000 names on my computer. Now, I don't use them all the time. But the more usable the information you have provided me, the more likely I am to call on you the next time.

Business in the 90s is relationship building. And it's a slow process. And it's certainly easier to destroy than to build up. It's that plodding, step-by-step approach to getting publicity and being a consultant.

REECE: Thanks, Jan.

APPENDIX 9

Templates and Examples

ANNOUNCEMENT OF NEW CONSULTANCY— PRESS RELEASE TEMPLATE

For Immediate Release
[Contact's Name]
[Contact's Phone Number]
[Contact's Fax Number]

[YOUR NAME] OPENS NEW CONSULTING PRACTICE TO HELP SOLVE LOCAL [INSERT COMMON PROBLEM CLIENTS WILL HAVE] PROBLEMS

[City, State]—[Today's Date]—[Your company name or your name] has opened a [type of practice] consulting practice to help [your main target market] achieve [primary benefit they get from your help]. The practice is located at [your address] in [your city and state].

"[Quote—why clients will want to use you]," said [your name], who [list primary qualifications] and [list secondary qualifications]. "[Second quote on how you'll solve the problem stated]."

The company will provide [list primary services] and [list secondary services] so that clients can [list main benefits to clients].

[List other qualifications and credentials]

Call [your phone number] for a free half-hour consultation to [what they'll get from the freebie].

ANNOUNCEMENT OF NEW CONSULTANCY— PRESS RELEASE EXAMPLE

For Immediate Release
Reece Franklin
(909) 393-8634
(909) 393-8525 (Fax)

REECE FRANKLIN OPENS NEW CONSULTING PRACTICE TO HELP SOLVE LOCAL RETAILERS PROBLEM

(Chino, CA)—January 27, 2001—Reece Franklin and Associates has opened a small-business marketing consulting practice to help local retailers achieve a 20% increase in profits for the year 2001 and beyond. The practice is located at 19999 Central Avenue, Chino, CA.

"Retailers have been having a rough time during the last decade due to increased government regulation and user fees," said Mr. Franklin, who holds a BA from Northern Illinois University and has owned several small retail stores. "Through our background, we have identified over 25 new ways a small retailer can market their business successfully with little or no budget increase and still gain almost 210% profitability," continued Franklin.

The company will provide affordable marketing and advertising services so that clients can get all their promotion problems solved in a one-stop shopping atmosphere.

Franklin is a member of the Chino Valley Chamber of Commerce, and is the Chairman of the Chaffey College Small Business Task Force.

Call (909) 393-8525 for a free half-hour marketing audit and evaluation.

ANNOUNCEMENT OF NEW LOCATION MOVE FOR CONSULTANCY—TEMPLATE

For Immediate Release
[Contact's name]
[Contact's phone number]
[Contact's fax number]
[YOUR PRACTICE NAME] MOVES LOCATION TO [NEW CITY], CONSULTANT SAYS MORE BUSINESSES HAVE [MAIN PROBLEM] PROBLEMS THAT NEED ADDRESSING
[New City, State]—[Today's date]—[Your company name or your name] has moved their [type of practice] practice to [new city]. The new address is [insert address].

"[Quote—what new main problem is, and why you want to help solve it]," said [your name], owner of [company name], previously in [old city name].

The company will still provide [list primary services] services to [list target audience], but on a much wider scale. With their history of solving [list main problem] problems, the company felt it was time to tackle the problems in [list new city].

"[Quote on what clients will gain from the move]," said [your name], owner of [company name].

The company provides [list primary services] and [list secondary services] to [list target audiences].

[List any qualifications, awards, or major recognitions from old city.]

Call [your phone number] for a free half-hour consultation to [what they'll get from the freebie].

ANNOUNCEMENT OF NEW LOCATION MOVE FOR CONSULTANCY—EXAMPLE

For Immediate Release
Reece Franklin
(909) 393-8634
(909) 393-8525 (Fax)

REECE FRANKLIN & ASSOCIATES MOVES LOCATION TO ONTARIO, CONSULTANT SAYS MORE BUSINESSES HAVE GROWTH PROBLEMS THAN EVER BEFORE

(Ontario, CA)—(October 31, 2001)—Reece Franklin & Associates has moved their marketing practice to Ontario, CA. The new address is 1234 Main Street, Suite 5B, Ontario, CA 99999.

"Most small businesses are having tremendous growth problems," said Reece Franklin, owner. "As a small business myself, I know the frustrations they're feeling. I believe it's time to jump start a new program."

To this end, Franklin has developed a new workshop entitled "How To Grow Your Business into the Next Millenium." The first seminar in a series called the Small Business Growth Academy, it will be held at the Ontario Chamber of Commerce, 5599 Main Street, Ontario, on July 15th, 1996.

Franklin stressed that his company still provides marketing and advertising services to small companies with under 100 employees but is expanding to a much wider audience. With their history of solving particularly perplexing marketing problems, the company felt it was time to tackle the problems in Ontario.

"Clients in Ontario will gain an understanding of what to do with a quick, simple, and effective ten-step approach to new marketing," said Franklin.

Reece Franklin and Associates are the recipients of the Golden Eye Award from the American Marketing Association, Inland Empire Chapter, and received the "Business of The Year" Status from the Chino Valley Chamber of Commerce.

Franklin is offering a free half-hour business check-up prior to the main seminar. To register, call 909-393-8525.

CONSULTANT'S SERVICE FACT SHEET

For Further Information, Contact
[Your name]
[Your phone number]
[Your fax number]

FACT SHEET—[COMPANY NAME]

WHO: [Company Name]
WHAT: [Explain in One Graph What You Do]
WHERE: [Your Full Address]
WHEN: [Date(s) You Are Offering This Service]
WHY: [Explain Generally Why Your Consultancy Benefits the Client]
HOW: [Explain Specifically How It Benefits Them]

ANNOUNCEMENT OF NEW CONTRACT—PRESS RELEASE TEMPLATE

For Immediate Release

[Contact name]
[Phone number]
[Fax number]

[YOUR COMPANY NAME] AWARDED [NAME OF CLIENT] CONTRACT

[City, State]—[Today's date]—[Your company name] [short description of what you do], announced today the award of a contract with [name of new client], to provide [list one or two major services you will provide].

"[Quote on why you're happy to be associated with new client.]"

[Name of new client] has been in business since [list year of client's start up] as the [list their main service or product]. [List reason they're looking to you for help.]

[Insert standard paragraph about your company, and services you provide.]

For further information, contact [your name] at [your phone number].

ANNOUNCEMENT OF NEW CONTRACT—PRESS RELEASE EXAMPLE

For Immediate Release
Reece Franklin
(909) 393-8634
(909) 393-8525 (Fax)

REECE FRANKLIN AND ASSOCIATES AWARDED NEW DEL FAIR CONTRACT

(Ontario, CA)—(October 31, 2001)—Reece Franklin and Associates, marketing consultants to small business, announced today the award of a contract with the Del Fair to provide marketing and support services for the annual $15 million event.

"We are very proud to be associated with one of the longest running and most prestigious of all annual county fairs," said company spokesperson Dee Fox. "The Del Fair has long been considered the number-one fair in North America. We're excited to be able to help them launch their new look for the next century and beyond."

The Del Fair has been running continuously since 1908, when it started as an agricultural county fair and livestock show. Over the years the attendance has dropped, which caused fair management to look for a new marketing company.

Reece Franklin and Associates is a full-service marketing and advertising firm specializing in fair and event planning. Located in Ontario, CA, they've been instrumental in event turn-around since their founding in 2001.

For further information, contact Reece Franklin at 909-393-8525.

SPECIAL EVENT—PRESS RELEASE TEMPLATE

For Immediate Release
[Contact name]
[Phone Number]
[Fax Number]

[Your company] TO (HOST, HOLD, COORDINATE) [Insert major event]

[Your city, state]—[Today's date]—[Your company name], [short description of what you do], has been picked to (host, hold, coordinate) the [insert major event]. The event will be held [day, date] at [full location address].

"[Quote about how delighted you are to be able to donate your time for this major event]."

[Your company] stressed the need for all [insert target audience] to participate. "[Quote on why local target audience should be involved.]"

For further information, contact the [charity or event organization] at [phone number].

SPECIAL EVENT—PRESS RELEASE EXAMPLE

For Immediate Release

Reece Franklin

(909) 393-8634

(909) 393-8525 (Fax)

REECE FRANKLIN & ASSOCIATES TO COORDINATE ANNUAL LABOR DAY MDA TELETHON

(Chino, CA)—(August 12, 1993)—Reece Franklin and Associates, local marketing and advertising consultancy, has been picked to coordinate the local portion of the annual Jerry Lewis Labor Day Muscular Dystrophy Telethon for the Inland Empire. Local facilities will emanate from the Chino Promenade Shopping Center, Central at Philadelphia, downtown Chino.

"We are delighted Reece Franklin and Associates has generously donated their time to help us," said Sandra Sabul, local MDA District Director. "Their company has been involved with MDA since 1970 and always provides us the expertise we need to reach our goals."

Franklin stresses the need for all local businesses to participate. "Local Chino Valley business should make this charity a number-one priority," he stated. "We're so close to finding a cure. This could be the year their help puts us over the top."

For further information, contact the Muscular Dystrophy Association at (090) 777-8888.

CONSULTANT'S AWARD RECIPIENT— PRESS RELEASE TEMPLATE

For Immediate Release

[Contact name]

[Phone number]

[Fax number]

[Your name] WINS PRESTIGIOUS [Award name] FROM [Who awarded to you]

[Your city, state]—[Today's date]—[Your name], owner of [your company name], a [description of business] consultancy, has been awarded the prestigious [name of award] by the [awarding group]. The award was presented [where, what, and when].

In accepting the award, [your name] [statement praising group for recognition]. "[Quote on how group helped you achieve mutual goals]."

[Your name] cited statistics showing [use target audience, showing how they have problem you are able to solve].

[Paragraph on what your company does for the target audience defined above.]

CONSULTANT'S AWARD RECIPIENT— PRESS RELEASE EXAMPLE

For Immediate Release
Reece Franklin
(909) 393-8634
(909) 393-8525 (Fax)

REECE FRANKLIN WINS PRESTIGIOUS "SMALL BUSINESSMAN" AWARD FROM CHINO CHAMBER

(Chino, CA)—(October 20, 1998)—Reece Franklin, owner of MarketSmarts, a small-business marketing consultancy, has been awarded the prestigious "Small Business Medal of Merit" by the Chino Chamber of Commerce. The award was presented at a chamber business-to-business luncheon held on Friday, October 9.

In accepting the award, Franklin praised his fellow members of the Chamber Small Business Committee. "Without their courage and dedication, the ability of small business in the area to thrive through these economic hard times would be impossible," said Franklin.

Franklin cited statistics showing one of every two small businesses that opened in the beginning of 1996 was already closed. He stressed the need for continuing small business education and praised the opening of the recent Institute of Continuing Business Education Center at the Chamber offices.

MarketSmarts, a full-service marketing and advertising firm, specializes in small-to-medium-sized businesses of under 100 employees. They are located at 14144 Central Avenue, Suite G, Chino, CA 91810.

For further information, contact Reece Franklin at 909-393-8525.

SAMPLE SPEAKER'S BIOGRAPHY

[Your name in caps]   [Insert pic]

[Your name] has been called the "guru" of [your specialty] by the [insert media that's given you status, or client group that has]. (He, She) is recognized as an innovator in teaching [your specialty, reworded] to over [number of clients you've had] in [your state] since [year you started consulting].

(His, Her) audiences range from business conferences to associations and trade organizations, from [give range of numbers in audience] at a time. Some of [your name]'s clients include: [list prestigious clients only].

Topics include [list top four or five topics for speeches].

[Your name] began (his, her) career as a [specialty] in [year] and moved into [next specialty] in [year]. Before establishing the company in [year], [first name] was [list last three major titles when employed].

(He, She) has been featured in [list major publications that have run your articles, articles about you, or reviews of your book(s)]. [First name] is the author of [list title(s)].

[First name] is a member of [list memberships].

[First name] was educated at [list college(s)], and holds a [list degree(s)].

CONSULTANT'S SPEAKING ONE-SHEET

[Your name in caps]   [Insert pic]

[Slogan relating to client base]

[Your name] is a successful entrepreneur with a background in [list specialties]. (He, She) brings many talents to the platform in over [insert number of speeches per year] presentations per year.

[Your first name] will share (his, her) techniques, triumphs, and thought-provoking stories with your members in a humorous and human manner.

Your audience will learn real world techniques they can apply to their situation IMMEDIATELY!

ORGANIZATIONS THAT HAVE FEATURED [YOUR NAME]:
[List 6 to 12 groups you've spoken before.]
AFFILIATIONS:
[List all groups you belong to that apply to this one sheet.]
TOPICS:
[List in priority order the speech titles you give. Follow each with a one-sentence description of the topic.]
KEYNOTES—WORKSHOPS—SEMINARS—CUSTOM PROGRAMS—IN-HOUSE TRAINING
[Your company name] [Company mailing address and phone]

CONSULTANT'S SPEECH ANNOUNCEMENT—PRESS RELEASE TEMPLATE

For Immediate Release
[Contact name]
[Phone number]
[Fax number]

[Your specialty] CONSULTANT TO SPEAK AT [list event] [OR]
[Your specialty] CONSULTANT TO SHOW [List target audience] HOW TO [What you do]

[Your city, state]—[Today's date]—[Your name, your company], a [your city]-based [your specialty], will speak at the [name of event] on [day, date and time] at the [full location address]. [Your name] topic will be [insert title of speech].

"[Quote on the main problem your audience has, and how your speech will show them how to solve it]."

The presentation will focus on three key principles: [list three keys you intend to use as your speech].

For reservations, contact [insert contact name] at [contact's phone number].

CONSULTANT'S SPEECH ANNOUNCEMENT— PRESS RELEASE EXAMPLE

For Immediate Release
Reece Franklin
(909) 393-8634
(909) 393-8525 (Fax)

MARKETING CONSULTANT TO SHOW MAJOR SAN DIEGO CORPORATIONS HOW TO "WRITE IT RIGHT!"

(San Diego, CA)—(October 1, 1995)—Reece Franklin, owner of MarketSmarts, a Chino-based small business marketing consultant, will speak at the annual San Diego IRC (Industrial Recreation Council) convention on Thursday, October 12, 1995, 1 p.m. at the Point Loma Naval Club. Mr. Franklin's speech topic is "Write It Right!—Why Executives Can't Write."

"Most executives get caught up in the merry-go-round of using $500 words when they could just as easily use $50 words and get the message across in half the time," said Franklin. "This speech will teach them how to put together an easy-to-understand memo or sales letter in half the usual time," he continued.

The presentation will focus on three key principles: seven steps to writing right, how to outline the 60-second memo, and how to create a must-read sales letter or proposal, all chapters in Franklin's new book *Write It Right!*, AAJA Press, 1995.

For reservations, contact Bill Doremus at 619-555-1212.

CONSULTANT'S BOOK CONTRACT— PRESS RELEASE TEMPLATE

For Immediate Release
[Contact name]
[Phone number]
[Fax number]

LOCAL CONSULTANT SIGNS WITH [Insert regional or national] PUBLISHER TO AUTHOR [Insert subject] BOOKS

[Your city, state]—[Today's date]—[Local or regional] [type of consultant you are] consultant and author [your name], has signed a contract to write the first of several books for [insert publisher's name]. The first book, [insert book title], is scheduled to be published in [insert pub date].

"[Quote on how delighted you are to work with publisher, and why]."

[Your name]'s book takes a look at the [insert subject of book]. "[Quote on why this book is different from others]."

Chapters include information on [list three hot chapters].

For further information, contact [your name] at [phone number].

CONSULTANT'S BOOK CONTRACT— PRESS RELEASE EXAMPLE

For Immediate Release

Reece Franklin

(909) 393-8634

(909) 393-8525 (Fax)

LOCAL CONSULTANT SIGNS WITH MAJOR NY PUBLISHER TO AUTHOR PR BOOK

(Chino, CA)—(October 1, 1995)—Local marketing consultant and author Reece Franklin, Reece Franklin and Associates, has signed a contract to write the first of several books for John Wiley and Sons, New York. The first book, *Consultant's Guide to Publicity,* is scheduled to be published in the spring of 1996.

"I'm delighted to work with the editors at Wiley," said Franklin. "They have a long history (since 1807) of turning out excellent business books. And they understand how to work with consultants, having their own specific consultant's book division," he continued.

Franklin's book takes a look at the ins and outs of publicity for consultants as seen through the eyes of a consultant himself. "Product publicity is entirely different than that for a service business, such as a consultant," quoted Franklin. "That's why this book is so important."

Chapters include information on what makes a good story idea, developing good media relations, how to write a winning press release, and more.

For further information, contact Reece Franklin at 909-393-8525.

AUTHOR'S BOOK BIOGRAPHY

[On your letterhead]
AUTHOR AVAILABLE FOR INTERVIEWS
[Start with quote about what your happy-camper clients call you—genius, guru, etc.]

[List two or three quotes from local newspapers—what they call you.]

[List one or two quotes/testimonials from clients.]

SO WHO REALLY IS [Your Name]?

[Insert brief, one-paragraph biographical description of who you are, with a humanist approach.]

[Write one or two paragraphs about the book—how you came to write it, what it does for the readers, etc.]

[List four or five things that make you a *dynamic* guest.]

I am a [list three modifiers like energetic, enthusiastic, etc.] guest. I'd love to share my information with your readers, listeners, or viewers. Reaction is always high. To book an interview, call me at [insert phone number].

BOOK PRESS RELEASE

For Immediate Release
[Contact name]
[Phone number]
[Fax number]
[Name of book] REVEALS [Startling secret] ABOUT [Target audience]
[OR]
[Type of person you are] SAYS [Target audience] NEEDS HELP, PENS BOOK TO SOLVE THE PROBLEM IN HALF THE TIME

[Your city, state]—[Today's date]—[Your name], [Type of consultant] consultant, has released (his, her) new book, [title of book], published by [name of publisher].

This is the first book to [insert uniqueness that makes this the first book to do something relating to your consulting specialty]. While other books focus on [list general topic], [your name]'s book specifically focuses on [list primary hot button audience has].

According to [list organization or well-known expert in your field], this problem has been bothering [list target audience] for many years. [Title of book] is the first one to address these problems and offer positive solutions.

[Title of book] reveals: [list four or five topics that book focuses on—probably chapter heads].

[Your name] is a well-known [specialty] consultant, located in [your city, state]. (He, She) has been specializing in [specialty] since [date consultancy started] and has helped over [number of] clients.

[Title of book], ISBN [number] is [no. of pages] pages, [hardbound/paperbound], and retails for [retail price]. For further information, or to book an interview, call [your name] at [phone number].

BOOK FLYER

"[Quote from early review source]"   [Insert pix of cover]
IF YOU'VE GOT SOMETHING TO [What Service Does] . . .
HERE'S! THE BOOK THAT WILL SHOW YOU HOW
NOW LEARN HOW TO [What Your Clients Need to Do]
with These Simple, Low-Cost Methods That Work!
Dear Fellow [Target market],
[First paragraph—set up problems by stating questions such as "Are You frustrated with . . ."]

If these and other questions have you stumped, I have the answer.

INTRODUCING THE FIRST BOOK IN YEARS TO [Primary Benefit]

[Describe title of book, ISBN, and when published.]

DON'T MISS OUT!

[Small quote from other early review]

WHAT OTHERS ARE SAYING:

[Insert two or three testimonials from reviewers or readers.]

THESE TECHNIQUES REALLY WORK!

[Two graphs on how these techniques work]

SOME SPECIFIC EXAMPLES:

[Give three quick client case histories.]

TABLE OF CONTENTS

[Insert book TOC.]

MY UNCONDITIONAL GUARANTEE! If for ANY REASON, WHATSOEVER, you are not completely satisfied with this book, return your copy to me within 10 days, in resellable condition, and I'll give you your money back. No questions asked. It's that simple—'cause I want you to be happy!

[Insert order form here]

CONSULTANT'S BOOK DEBUT— PRESS RELEASE TEMPLATE

For Immediate Release
[Contact name]
[Phone number]
[Fax number]

LOCAL CONSULTANT'S BOOK ON [Subject] TO DEBUT AT [Insert location or event] THIS [Insert timeline]

[Your city, state]—[Today's date]—[Your name], local [type of consulting you do] consultant and author, announced the publishing of (his, her) [which book] book from [insert publisher's name], the [book title]. The debut will take place at [insert book event] on [day/date/time] at [location] [address].

"[Quote on how excited you are about book launch, and why]."

[Your name] is also the author of [list any other books, booklets, cassettes or videos you've produced].

[Place of event] is located at [insert location address].

For further information, contact [your name] at [phone number].

CONSULTANT'S BOOK DEBUT— PRESS RELEASE EXAMPLE

For Immediate Release
Reece Franklin
(909) 393-8634
(909) 393-8525 (Fax)

LOCAL CONSULTANT'S BOOK ON PUBLICITY TO DEBUT AT AUTOGRAPH PARTY THIS WEEK

(Chino, CA)—(April 14, 1996)—Reece Franklin, local marketing consultant and author, announced the publishing of his first book from John Wiley and Sons, NY, the *Consultant's Guide to Publicity*. The debut will take place at a book signing and autograph party Friday, April 19, 1996 at Majestic Coffee, Chino Hills Marketplace, Chino Hills, from 5 p.m. to 9 p.m.

"I'm really excited to launch the book tour here in my hometown," said Franklin. "We've invited every major business owner to come to the party and receive a complementary excerpt chapter from the book. And of course, we'll hold informal discussions on what publicity tactics they've used and how they can improve them."

Franklin is also the author of *Inventor's Marketing Handbook* (AAJA) and *How To Sell and Promote Your Project, Idea or Invention* (Prima).

Majestic Coffee is located at 4120 Chino Hills Parkway, in the Chino Hills Marketplace, next to China Palace.

For further information, contact Reece Franklin at 909-393-8525.

REVIEWER'S FACT SHEET FROM BOOK-REVIEW PACKAGE

[on your letterhead]
REVIEWER'S FACT SHEET
[Title of book]

[Publication date]	ISBN [Number]
[Shipping date]	[Page Count; Price]
	[Backmatter—glossary, index, etc.]

BLURB

[Title of book] is the [description in one sentence about what book is about]. For anyone who has been [list target audience], this book is for them.

Author [your name], a [type of business] consultant, takes a look at [general description of book].

Table of Contents

[List chapter titles.]

PUBLICITY PLANS

[Insert any lecture tours, books signings, articles, radio or TV interview tours, etc.]

SAMPLE QUESTION-AND-ANSWER FORM

Q1.   Why did you write this book?

A1.   [Insert reason]

Q2.   What's different about this book from others on the market?

A2.   [Insert answer]

Q3.   What makes you an expert in [your field]?

A3.   [Insert answer]

Q4.   Can you give us a few examples of how these techniques work?

A4.   [Insert two or three quick case histories]

Q5.   Where can our (listeners, viewers, readers) get the book?

A5.   [Insert fulfillment information]

SEMINARS OFFERED BY REECE A. FRANKLIN

INVENTOR'S MARKETING WORKSHOP

An intensive one-day course based on the book *How to Sell and Promote Your Idea, Project, or Invention.* Includes sessions on idea generation, prototypes, patents, trademarks, copyrights, financing and budgeting, selling out for big profits, selling to the U.S. government, marketing, public relations, advertising, trade show marketing, networking—and more! Now that you've bought the book, take the seminar for some hands-on instruction tailored to *your* invention!

HOW TO GET FREE PUBLICITY

Number One on the hit parade of seminar attendees the past five years in a row! Greatly expanded and revised, with supplemental information from local media sources. Perfect for small businesses and nonprofits. Half day or full day. Topics include news release preparation, elements of a press kit, how to book radio and television interviews, making editors want your information, dealing effectively with the media—and more!

HOW TO ADVERTISE AND PROMOTE YOUR SMALL BUSINESS

This one-day, intensive seminar is designed for those small businesses who realize the need for *effective* advertising and promotion plans but don't know where to start. Topics include the elements of a good ad, how to set up an ad budget, how to get *more* from your ad space, which media to use and why, cost-effective promotions that work, how to get *free* layout design and artwork—and more!

DESIGNING EFFECTIVE SMALL BUSINESS ADS

This course, offered in response to student requests, gives you everything you need to design ads that work. This half-day, intensive workshop includes producing eye-catching ads that sell, the basic tools for success, how to write good ad copy, how to write headlines that make money, how to upgrade your company image using small space effectively—and more!

For complete information on these seminars or on how I can help you with your idea, project, or invention, contact me:
Reece Franklin and Associates
P.O. Box 2667
Chino, CA 91708-2667
(909) 393-8525

About the Author

Reece Franklin runs MarketSmarts, a marketing, advertising, and public relations firm. He has done publicity campaigns for dozens of entrepreneurs and consultants. He gives more than one hundred seminars annually, with titles such as *Publicity for Consultants, How to Advertise and Promote Your Consulting, Business Writing for Consultants,* and *Advanced Marketing Tactics for Consultants.* Franklin also teaches a class, "How to Get Free Publicity," at more than thirty California colleges. He has been featured in *Inc., Entrepreneur Magazine,* and many other business publications. Franklin has penned several books, including *The Consultant's Guide to Publicity, Inventor's Marketing Handbook,* and *How to Market Your Home-Based Business.*

For complete information on Reece Franklin seminars, workshops, books, and consulting services, he can be contacted at:

MarketSmarts
P.O. Box 2667
Chino, California 91708-2667
(909) 393-8525

Credits

Grateful acknowledgment is given to the following publications and authors for generous permission to reprint from the appropriate sources:

Page 14—Cons of Publicity—Reprinted by permission of The Putnam Publishing Group/Jeremy P. Tarcher, Inc. From *Getting Business to Come to You* by Paul and Sarah Edwards and Laura Clampitt Douglas. Copyright © 1991 by Paul and Sarah Edwards.

Figure 3-2. © 1994 & 1988 by Gloria Michels from the book *How to Make Yourself Famous,* published by Hastings House.

Figure 5-10. Specific articles reprinted by permission of *Inland Daily Bulletin, Northern Star, Bakersfield Californian, Orange Coast Daily Pilot,* and *Chino Champion.*

Figure 5-11. Reprinted with permission from *Entrepreneur Magazine,* June 1992.

Figures 5-13, 5-21. Reprinted with permission of Marie Reichelt, ABP Associates.

Figure 5-14. Reprinted with permission of Postal Annex.

Figure 5-15. Reprinted with permission of Linda Pinson.

Figure 5-19. Reprinted with permission of *The Orange County Register,* copyright 1992.

Figure 5-25. Reprinted with permission of *Inc.* Magazine, August 1992. Copyright 1992 by Goldhirsh Group, Inc., 38 Commercial Wharf, Boston, MA 02110.

Figure 5-29. Reprinted with permission of *Inland Daily Bulletin,* April 1994.

Figure 5-30. Reviews reprinted with permission of *Library Journal,* Cahners, January 1990, and Pat Wagner, *Pattern Research* and *Bloomsbury Review,* March 1990.

Figure 6-4. Reprinted with permission of Freedom To Fly, copyright 1993.

Page 125—Description of pilot system. Reprinted from the book *Self-Publishing Manual,* 8th Edition, by Dan Poynter, Para Publishing, 1996.

Page 159—Radio Talk Show System. Reprinted with permission of Joe and Judy Sabah.

Appendix 1. Reprinted from "How To Prepare and Market Articles That Sell" from the book *How to Sell More than 75% of Your Freelance Writing* by Gordon Lee Burgett, Prima, 1995.

Appendix 2. Reprinted from "How To Study a Magazine Article" from the book *How to Sell More than 75% of Your Freelance Writing* by Gordon Lee Burgett, Prima, 1995.

Appendix 3. Reprinted from the book *Query Letters, Cover Letters* by Gordon Lee Burgett, Communications Unlimited, 1985.

Appendix 4. Reprinted with permission of Jan Norman.

Appendix 8. Reprinted with permission of Jan Norman and Reece Franklin.

Index

INDEX

INDEX

INDEX